FREE

FREE

Build an Online Following that
Liberates You for Life's Adventures

LINDA CLAIRE PUIG

MIRASEE PRESS

5750 Avenue Notre Dame de Grace
Montreal, Quebec
H4A 1M4, Canada
www.mirasee.com

Paperback ISBN: 978-1-7347725-5-5
E-book ISBN: 978-1-7347725-6-2

1 3 5 7 9 10 8 6 4 2

To my son, who made motherhood the adventure of a lifetime.

CONTENTS

INTRODUCTION

I'M STANDING on a tiny 3-foot by 3-foot trapeze platform 35 feet in the air. Safety lines are attached to loops on both sides of my flyer's belt, and a very muscular instructor known as the Line Puller is on the ground holding onto them.

I've been told that Mr. Line Puller will *never let go of these lines*, and if anything funny happens when I'm flying, he *will not let me fall*.

My other instructor, known as the Board Biscuit, is on the platform with me, her own belt hooked onto the rigging and her right arm wrapped around my waist for added reassurance. She hands me the chalk bag so I can chalk up to avoid sweaty, slippery hands. I'm wishing I could "chalk up" my pounding heart!

The trapeze bar swings toward us and Ms. Board Biscuit uses a hook to reel it in. At her direction, I lean out over the platform and grab the bar with my right hand. Mind you, she's still holding

1

me around the waist and Mr. Line Puller is still attentively holding the safety lines down on the precious ground. Plus my left hand is clenched onto the nearby rig cable.

So at least for the moment, I'm not going to die.

But then Ms. Board Biscuit tells me it's time to grab the bar with both hands. Which means I've got to release my left hand's death grip on the rig cable.

It's the moment of full commitment. Once both hands are on the bar, my whole body will be leaning out over the net—35 feet off the ground. Ms. Board Biscuit, hanging onto the back of my safety belt now, will be the only thing keeping me from plunging right off the platform.

She will soon yell, "Ready!" at which time I am to bend my knees. Then she'll yell, "Hep!" and I am to jump off of the platform and...fly.

Except I can't get my left hand to unclench and let go of the rig cable.

"You can do it," she says. "I've got you."

Fear has me in tunnel vision. My entire being is focused on my left hand and its knuckles, white because of the tight grip.

I can do this, I think, trying to convince myself.

Finally, I take a deep breath, release my hand from the security of the cable, and watch as my hand slowly arcs up and over to the bar. *Very, very* slowly. It feels as if it takes five minutes for that hand to reach the bar.

"Ready!"

I bend my knees.

"Hep!"

I fly.

Years later, I thought of this experience as my hand arced in slow motion toward the send button on my very first email newsletter to about 200 people.

Though I knew I was "supposed to" do a newsletter, I didn't want to send it. I'd written hundreds of client newsletters before, but this felt *very* different. For one thing, those were print newsletters. Somehow, sending to a person's inbox felt more intimate. And I felt more vulnerable, more exposed.

The biggest difference, though, was that now I was writing for myself and for my own business. I was marketing ME. And unlike while working for clients, I was now wracked with uncertainty and fear.

Do I really know anything that my audience doesn't already know? Will the technology really work or am I just sending into a black Internet hole? Will it be any good?

It was a toxic stew that cooked just beneath my consciousness. And it got me.

Like it gets far too many solopreneurs and small business owners with good and important work to share.

I hit send. But I didn't send another newsletter for six months. And then not until six months after that. It went on like that for a few years.

My efforts to grow my online audience and add clients went in similar fits and starts. As I watched early leaders host list-building webinars and virtual speaker summits and make email offers, I added subscribers mainly by attending conferences in person, two or three a year. Not a terrible way to go about it, but definitely slow and *very* expensive.

And even though I'd met my new subscribers in person, the sparse emails that I sent were from *my company*, not from me. They were institutional. I figured, if a *company* made a mistake or promoted its offerings or pissed people off—well, I could still hide out.

Slowly, slowly, just like that left hand arcing toward the trapeze bar, I grew aware of the power of showing up, personally, in my emails. Which, of course, cranked up the fear when I started doing just that.

I also began to realize that if I really wanted to create the freedom I envisioned for my life through my business, I needed to take a deep breath and fully commit to building an online audience and developing an authentic, mutually beneficial relationship with them. I needed to recognize the value of what I knew and share it. I needed to put more of *me* into it. I needed to power through the fear.

So in late 2007, I jumped.

"Hep!"

And I flew! Since then, I've built a responsive international audience and made millions—all online. I've grown comfortable conducting large online "launches," teaching webinars, and hosting list-building events. I've become a recognized expert in developing authentic, profitable relationships via email. I'm a top collaborative partner with many of the leaders in my industry. It no longer scares me to send emails, even very personal ones. And I no longer fret about what people think of me.

On the personal side, because of my online audience, I'm able to call the shots on when and where I work. I was able to be superpresent as a single mom until my son went off to college. I was able to spend weeks nursing my mother in Texas after two knee surgeries. I never have to say no to meeting a friend or talking with a family member.

So, yay! Progress!

But building my audience and nurturing the relationship has made possible something even deeper and more profound than all of that goodness. Something life-changing.

I am *living* my heart's desire. I am free.

As I write this, the whole world is "grounded" because of the COVID-19 pandemic. But this time last year, I was in Sydney, Australia, for a month, then New Zealand. Before that, I drove across Canada with a friend, celebrated my birthday during a month in Prague, and before that, met new friends in Barcelona and Morocco. That was just 2019.

In the past six years alone, I've spent quality time in 27 countries. I learned to tango in Buenos Aires, to relax in Uruguay. I witnessed a hillside covered in crosses in Lithuania, the mind-blowing aurora borealis in Norway, and the grandeur of Moscow and St. Petersburg in Russia. I learned Italian from a Ukrainian (go figure!) while living in Italy for half a year, and motorcycled through the rice fields and temples of the Balinese countryside. I burst into tears as a 400-person chorus began Handel's *Messiah* inside the Sydney Opera House—and into cheers at Sydney's New Year's Eve fireworks.

It is my dream life. It's not about racing through "sites" and museums; it's about living for weeks, sometimes even months at a time in another locale—lingering, tasting what it's like to live there, to be from there. It nourishes my soul and makes me feel alive!

Being able to live this dream life is a direct result of building and nurturing an authentic relationship with an online audience of potential clients, some of whom buy my programs and services. I call them my "freedom following."

Your dreams might be different from mine (I have a friend who hates travel and wants to raise horses). Your audience will be different from mine. Doesn't matter. If you want your business to fund your vision of freedom, the key to unlock it is your audience.

One of my favorite passages about the power of decisions is by W.H. Murray, author of *The Scottish Himalayan Expedition,* which was published in 1951.

> *Concerning all acts of initiative (and creation), there is one elementary truth, the ignorance of which kills countless ideas and splendid plans: that the moment one definitely commits oneself, then Providence moves too. All sorts of things occur to help one that would never otherwise have occurred. A whole stream of events issues from the decision, raising in one's favour all manner of unforeseen incidents and meetings and material assistance, which no man could have dreamt would have come his way.*

In other words, until you *decide*, nothing will change. But once you decide, magic happens.

That's why I'm writing this book: to help you *decide* and to help you attract and nurture your own online audience. Because doing so will set you free.

• • •

The concept of using the Internet to get in front of your ideal clients isn't new. It's basically about finding and staying in touch online with people who might want or need what you have to offer. You've probably heard it a million times:

Grow your list!
Connect with your tribe!

Engage your people!
Content marketing this...
Relationship marketing that...

Google the topic and you'll find more blog posts, articles, and courses than you could take in over a whole year. They'll tell you that Facebook groups and/or Facebook Live are the answer. And LinkedIn and Instagram and Pinterest. They'll promise that YouTube is the gold mine. And joint ventures and large online events and blogs.

There's so much information—some of it good, plenty of it not—and so many different ways to build and engage an audience, that it can be extremely confusing and quite overwhelming.

Because of that, most people either do nothing or try to do everything. You'll put your efforts off for some imaginary day when you finally know it all. Or when you feel less nervous. Or you'll throw yourself into it and try *all* of the latest tricks and tactics and, most likely, not do any of them well.

And, of course, neither of those is going to set you free to fly in your business.

The good news is there are two big—and very common—mistakes that underlie this everything-or-nothing conundrum, mistakes this book will help you correct.

The first is not knowing who you want to work with—who they *really* are. Most of my students and clients have a general inkling of who their ideal clients are, sometimes little more than a vague notion. ("What I do can help *everyone!*?") Others *think* they know, but scratch the surface and their clarity is not nearly as deep and detailed as it needs to be.

The second mistake is not utilizing the attract-and-nurture audience tactic that's right for *you*. There's a mistaken belief that if, for example, other solopreneurs are crushing it with YouTube, you should be using it too. If well-known trainers say Facebook groups are where it's at, then you should be doing those as well.

But *should* you be doing Facebook groups? *Should* you be doing YouTube videos? Or let me put the emphasis differently. Should *you* be doing Facebook groups and YouTube videos? Is it possible to have the freedom you envision for yourself if you don't?

In a word, yes.

When you know your ideal clients deeply, and you choose your attraction and nurture strategies deliberately and perceptively, you create the map that leads to *your* treasure. No one else will have the same map. Because no one else is *you*.

• • •

So how will this book help? Part 1, "Free to..." begins with a closer look at five different types of freedom. What do these versions of freedom enable you to do? You'll be free to do *what*? You might be surprised to see how many ways freedom (or lack thereof) shapes our life.

Chapter 2, "The Secret," looks at *how* and *why* your audience is the key to that freedom, while Chapter 3, "Breaking Free," details the internal blocks to growing and nurturing an online audience and suggests a variety of ways to bust through those blocks.

The remaining chapters of Part 1 ("Destination: Who," "Destination: Where," and "Destination: What") explore in depth the three key questions you'll need to answer about your audience:

1. What are their demographic and psychographic details, traits, and characteristics?
2. Where do you find the people in your audience?
3. What do you do when you find them?

Part 2, "Free for..." investigates the philosophy of leading with generosity, offering a new take on an old idea in Chapter 7, "The Economy of Generosity." To bring the philosophy of leading with generosity into practice, Chapter 8, "Grow Your Freedom Following," details how to use *free* to establish and grow your audience. Importantly, it helps you begin to discover the audience-building tactics that are right for you. Chapter 9, "Nurture and Convert Your Freedom Following," distinguishes how to apply some of those same tactics to nurture and convert your audience into paying clients, students, and customers.

Finally, Part 3, "Free from..." considers how your audience shelters you from the storms that can interrupt your smooth sailing, beginning with Chapter 10, which explores how to get (and stay) in action on your audience-building efforts. Chapter 11 studies how to find your voice, discover the power of the personal, and ensure your audience sticks around. And Chapter 12 looks at how a well-nurtured, growing audience can save you from the storms of business life (such as a pandemic).

Along the way, I'll share stories and examples from my own business, as well as from others. You'll find practical tips and down-to-earth suggestions to "right-size" your own audience efforts. You'll also find exercises at the end of each chapter so that you get into immediate action; this helps anchor the learning and set you up for successful implementation in your own business.

I encourage you to read through the book once for the big picture vision, and then drill down into the chapters, reading and then doing the exercises. My hope is you'll find the book useful, insightful, and perhaps inspirational on the way to setting yourself free.

By the way, you don't need to read this entire book before taking a step in the direction of your freedom. Accept the invitation on the next page right now!

ADDITIONAL SUPPORT FOR YOU!

REGISTER NOW FOR THE FREE 3-DAY

FREEDOM BUSINESS BOOTCAMP

READ THIS FIRST

To say thank you for reading my book and support your continued learning, I'd love for you to join me at my 3-day "Freedom Business Bootcamp," **April 6–8, 2021**. Get a jump start now to create your freedom business—at no cost whatsoever. It's my gift to you.

→ Go to **www.FreedomBusinessBootcamp.net** to register now.

PART 1

FREE TO…

Chapter 1
ON FREEDOM

"Freedom is not something that anybody can be given. Freedom is something people take, and people are as free as they want to be."
—JAMES BALDWIN

It happened as I was driving through Montefiascone, a lovely hilltop village in central Italy. I had been living in Italy for several months, and my mother and her friend, chatting happily in the back seat, had come to visit.

We'd just finished a leisurely lunch, and I decided to take a scenic route home, so I turned down a picturesque, cobblestone road that hugged the side of the hill as it curved around and down. I felt so excited to be having this experience!

The road was narrow, but there were at least a couple of feet on either side of the car, and I was confident it would open back up. It was kind of thrilling!

Little did I know...

This still picturesque (but now worrisome) road continued to get narrower and narrower, with nowhere to turn, just walls on either side that began getting taller and closing in on us.

I pulled the side mirrors in and contemplated backing out the way I'd come, but now the road was so narrow that going in reverse seemed scarier than going forward.

Still, I had no idea what to expect if I continued on. We now had about 1 inch on either side of the car. YIKES! We couldn't even have gotten out of the car at this point—not even from a window!

My mom and her friend were now silent, their faces white. I kept moving forward, HOPING that was my best option.

Suddenly, the road just ended. OH NO!

I couldn't imagine having to drive in reverse all that way, so I looked for some other way. My eyes landed on a narrow set of cobblestoned stairs to my right that cut through a manicured orchard. I knew what I had to do.

Without thinking another moment, I inched the car forward, BARELY managed to make the sharp right turn onto the staircase and then...very slowly...bumped my way down these stairs to the wide street below. WOOHOO!

Three men in police-looking uniforms standing guard outside a building gaped at me as I clunked down the stairs. I wondered if I'd get arrested....

This is the beginning of an email I used to promote a training program that I ran numerous times over a decade. The email went on to show how that experience mirrored the common path to business success. You start out thrilled to be in business, then things get a little scary and you're tempted to go back. You get to a place where you're no longer confident you'll succeed. You hit a dead end; you're stuck and looking around for help. The way shows itself, and even though you're not sure you can trust it, you move forward in faith and courage, bumpy terrain and all. In the end, that way leads to your freedom.

I like the story because it's dramatic and fun to tell, plus the email got consistently stellar open rates. The metaphors worked so well that a few people told me they joined my program *because* of that email! But I included it here because it illustrates the five different ways you can experience freedom when you have a well-nurtured, perfect-for-you audience that supports your thriving online business.

Location Freedom

From the beginning, I set my business up for location independence because I love, love, love to travel. It must be in my bones; my first trip abroad was at six months old, when my family moved to Germany for a few years.

My thirst for new places and people and food and languages is so strong that I want to be gone for long periods of time, to fully immerse myself. The trip to Italy referenced in the email above was an incredibly profound experience of that location freedom; altogether, I stayed nearly half a year in a small provincial town in between Rome and Tuscany. In 2016, I traveled nine months out of the year, including a delicious seven weeks in Buenos Aires, Argentina. There, I learned and danced tango every day of the week, all the while able to continue growing and supporting my online audience as they supported me.

I'm hardly the only entrepreneur to travel with my business—there's now a whole ecosystem set up around so-called "digital nomads," with housing and workspace and mixers. As I traveled, I discovered loads of other people taking advantage of this location freedom, being "on the road and making money." I hosted dozens of them in an online speaker series.

I even started a second business (AdventurousLife.io) bringing solopreneurs ages 40-plus with me to destinations around the world for a month at a time to live, work, and play. Ask any of them, and they'll describe a sense of "finding their family" with others who are nourished by the slow, sustained travel they're able to do—serving their clients and students, as their audience underwrites the thing that makes them feel alive.

Of course, location freedom is not just about international travel. When my mom had knee surgery one year, and again on the other knee the following year, I flew from California to Texas to be her "at-home nurse" as she healed. They were tender, sweet times. You don't get to do this when you are tethered to an office or struggling in your business because you haven't built an online audience that supports you.

Location freedom also looks like spending a month at your child's home, helping support him and his wife as they welcome their first child. Or helping build a Habitat for Humanity dwelling the next state over. Or training with a horse whisperer on a dude ranch. Or spending a week creating a series of list-building freebies in the mountains around Lake Tahoe. Or, or, or...

Bottom line: As you support and nurture your audience, they support your freedom.

And here's the most amazing thing: Your online audience *wants* you to travel to exciting places, wants you to hang out with your mom, wants you to build houses for those who need them, wants you to be mentored by the world's best horse whisperer. Why? Because you'll write about your experiences and they'll get to live and learn vicariously.

I used to think I shouldn't write about my travels—that doing so would look like bragging and would make others envious in a negative way. But I discovered a way to find the fitting metaphors so that I could be teaching while sharing, and my audience loved it! When I wrote about preparation and patience, from the perspective of waiting for the northern lights to start from a teensy tiny town in Norway, I was able to take the people on my list along with me. When I wrote the ridiculous story of getting stuck inside a closed-for-the-night department store in Rome, they ate it up—and learned a couple of valuable business tips, too.

Time Freedom

To me, time freedom means never having to say no. That's because what I can create for my audience to meet their needs is rarely tied to a time-certain. Well, okay, I do have to show up if I'm going to give a webinar, right? But otherwise, I can decide how to use my time, as long as I get done what I need to get done. No "office hours" for me!

A friend unexpectedly pops into town and wants to meet for midmorning coffee—I'm there! The sun is finally out after days of deluge—let's go for a coastal drive this afternoon. My son's going off to college—I'll take a week to drive him there and get him settled in and then another week at a mountain retreat to reorient to being an empty-nester. I can hop up and help Mom anytime when I'm her post-surgery nurse.

When time freedom meets location freedom, the possibilities get *really* interesting! In Europe, I can spend an entire day exploring the Christmas markets and holiday decorations in Paris, for example, and get work done later in the afternoon and evening when the time change means the United States is waking up and getting to it. In Argentina, I can take a long, vigorous walk through the gorgeous city, have a typical breakfast of medialunas and coffee, and get home and showered and ready for client calls first thing in the morning Pacific time.

Traveling through Australia, New Zealand, Bali, and Singapore was a little more challenging in terms of coordinating calls and meetings. Time changes involve adding a day and subtracting a few hours. But when your work consists of nurturing your audience or setting up audience growth funnels or loading up sale emails, you don't *need* to coordinate with other time zones. You can go on that magical motorbike ride through the Balinese countryside anytime you want!

Freedom to Choose

Developing an online audience that pays attention to you and buys your programs and services means you can choose your location. It means you can self-direct what you do with your time. But freedom of choice as it relates to audience is about so much more than that. It represents the ability to choose your own course of action and your own pattern of living, free from coercion and the controlling authority of others.

You are free to do what you love, free to call the shots, free to control your own future, free to work from home or from an office. Everything in your business is *your* choice.

You are free to impact people in the ways you choose. You choose who you serve, what you offer, how you price it. And this is important as you consider building and nurturing your audience because the options are numerous. Do you build a list of subscribers by giving webinars or offering an opt-in freebie? Do you keep in touch with and nurture your audience with video or photography or emails? As you'll see in Part 2, there is no one-size-fits-all answer. You get to choose how you build your audience and nourish the relationship, and I'll help you with that.

Underneath it all is the question of whether you want to build an empire with your business or a simplified one-person jam. You may feel excited at the prospect of stretching yourself to six and seven figures. Or your ambitions might be for a thriving solo act. I find too many entrepreneurs feel pressure to constantly "go big or go home!" You are free to choose, without justification.

Creative Freedom

Having your own audience-based online business means you'll wear a lot of hats, at least at first. There's no design department, no product development department, no copywriting department. It's all *you*!

And while this may sometimes feel like a curse, if you're honest with yourself, isn't it a little bit fun, even thrilling, to use your creativity in all these different "departments" of your business?

I remember fussing for hours to find just the right branding colors before I was established enough to hire a brand/website developer. And even then I probably got in their hair a little because it was so much fun!

The truth is, I could never have imagined I would feel so creatively fulfilled in my business. It was a blast being scriptwriter, location scout, and "talent" for the Italian-themed marketing videos I filmed for the launch of my 6-Figure Newsletter Secrets course. Putting together the speaker series I hosted for a couple of years, On the Road & Making Money, was enormously satisfying in every way. Writing my newsletters for years was a creative endeavor that helped me discover my voice.

Your audience supports you to find this creative expression—and they benefit from it!

Financial Freedom

Before quitting his job to devote 100% of his time to his online business, Tim had his utilities turned off and bills he couldn't pay. He recently sold a portfolio of websites for six figures.

Shane and his wife, Jocelyn, together brought home about $5,000 a month in 9-to-5 jobs they grew to really dislike. They started a business offering lesson plans, e-books, and other resources to teachers and now make millions.

Suzanne went from secretary to surpassing the seven-figure mark in a little more than three years.

You know that I could go on; you've heard stories like this, too. The Internet (and my own personal circle of friends and colleagues) is filled with wonderful stories of initial struggle to big bucks. I find them quite inspiring, though I know it takes a lot of hard work to get there.

Maybe you're not looking for your own rags-to-riches story. Not everyone wants a million-dollar business. But what I believe we can all agree on is that we want to be able to control our finances, not be controlled by them. We want to live debt-free and spend money on things that bring us joy. We want not to be stressed about life's financial decisions or emergencies. We want not to have to stay stuck in jobs we hate. We want to be able to fund the lifestyle we want, now and into retirement years. We want ease around money. We want financial freedom.

Fortunately, one of the very best routes to that financial freedom is an online business, one driven by an audience that trusts you to have the solutions to the problems they need help with and the support for the dreams they cherish.

The *Feeling* of Freedom

Let's go back to my story at the top of this chapter, the email that I wrote about driving down the stairs in Italy. I left you with three men in police-looking uniforms gaping at me. Here's how the email ended.

> *Three men in police-looking uniforms standing guard outside a building gaped at me as I clunked down the stairs. I wondered if I'd get arrested. But at this point, there was no stopping me!*

Finally...freedom!

FREEDOM!

This is sooooooo what tends to happen on the path to business success:

You start out thrilled to be in business, just like I was thrilled at first when I turned onto that gorgeous, cobblestoned street. It's all new, all pretty exciting, and you're filled with confidence that this is going to be a GREAT experience.

After a while, the path begins to get a little scary. You're tempted to go back to the way things were before you started your business. You keep inching forward, though now it's truly nerve-wracking, and you are no longer confident that you will succeed.

Then you hit a dead end. You feel stuck and you don't know what to do.

You need a way out. You need a staircase to freedom.

The email continued on to sell the course I was offering. But close your eyes a moment and just imagine the *feeling* of driving away after such an adventure in Italy, car intact, the three of us women hooting with glee—free!

This is my wish for you as you make your way through the concepts and steps in this book—the feeling of exhilaration that comes with having a successful audience-driven business. Your *audience* is your way out, your staircase to freedom. Read the next chapter to find out exactly why.

ACTION MOMENT

1. What type of freedom are you looking for?
2. If you had all the freedom you wanted, what would you do?
3. What's getting in the way of that freedom?

Chapter 2
THE SECRET

"Your audience gives you everything you need. They tell you. There is no director who can direct you like an audience."

—FANNY BRICE

A GUY I KNOW used to take pride in calling his business a "best-kept secret." It was a mysterious-sounding way to convey exclusivity, he thought, and he used the phrase almost as a calling card.

One day, with a conspiratorial glint in his eye, he again invoked the status of his company as a best-kept secret to a potential new client.

"That's your own damn fault," the prospect replied.

Ouch! What?

It was a whiplash moment, but it forced him to recognize that being a best-kept secret wasn't doing him *any* favors. In fact, it was holding him back. Being a best-kept secret meant everything was harder. Sure, his clients loved him, but adding to his client rolls or scaling his business to work one-to-many was a slog.

What he needed was a ready, online "audience"—an ever-growing group of people who pay attention to him, who understand how his business can help them, and who can see themselves maybe one day working with him. People he can stay in touch with regularly and make offers to occasionally, whenever he's ready to take on new clients or finally scale to that one-to-many approach.

In fact, the key to any and all of the entrepreneurial freedoms described in Chapter 1—financial, location, time, choice, and expression—is *audience*. Online audience. And before I go any further, let me define what I mean by "online audience" so there's no confusion.

Online Audience: A group of people you communicate with via online channels who are most likely to be interested in your products or services. They have a defined set of demographics and behaviors that makes them ideal for you, and you for them. You find these people in a variety of places, with the ultimate objective of getting them onto an email list so that you can communicate directly with them and build a profitable relationship. For purposes of this book, the terms *target market, niche,* and *ideal clients* are synonymous, even though there are ever-so-slight differentiations in their definitions. But don't get hung up on terms. "Audience" is what we're calling it.

Some people ask, "Why do I need an audience when I can just get traffic to my website?" Four short reasons:

1. Audiences are loyal; traffic is not.
2. Audiences make far more purchases than traffic does.
3. Audiences spread your message; traffic does not.
4. Audiences are less expensive than paid traffic.

Keywords and ads are more likely to attract website "tourists"—those who bop in for a quick look and head back out. And by quick, we're talking typically 10 seconds or less. *Just* like the tourists who snap a quick photo of the Leaning Tower of Pisa before rushing to the next "site." Unlike those tourists, a well-nurtured audience sticks around, sips cappuccino with you, becomes a local.

If you want to affect people's lives doing work you love—without working yourself to the bone—you need an audience. For your business to give you the freedom to call the shots, to name your hours, to go anywhere, anytime you choose—you need an audience. An audience you can reach and communicate with online. An audience of individuals you engage with authentically and honestly, a relationship you tend and nurture with as much care as you do your in-person relationships. An audience that self-selects when you open the door to new programs and services, so you don't ever have to strong-arm your sales.

An Audience-Driven Business

The first few years of my business, I ran a print newsletter service and kept in touch with my 50 or so clients individually by email. I ran ads in a national magazine and booked a booth at conferences around the country—wow, that was an expensive way to get new clients. And it felt like a slog to develop the kind of business I envisioned.

It wasn't until I actively started building an audience that business picked up. And the more I focused on developing my audience, the more I was able to do, to offer. I felt so fulfilled creatively and rewarded financially. I created my Ready2GoArticles.com site to help my audience keep in touch with *their* audience more easily. I created what became a hugely popular program, 6-Figure Newsletter Secrets, entirely while living in Italy—filming all my marketing videos in beautiful locations around the country. I filled my Portable Profits

Club coaching group and took them on retreats to Napa Valley, Italy, and the Bahamas. And tons more.

I couldn't have done *any* of it without a responsive, engaged audience with enough people in it to fill those kinds of offers. Just like it did for me, an audience-based business can open the doors for you to so many money-earning possibilities. Just a few examples:

- Coaching or therapy groups
- Books
- Done-for-you products/services
- Training courses, live and self-study
- Subscription services (e.g., beard grooming kit)
- Physical products of all kinds (e.g., card decks, dog collars)
- Virtual fitness classes
- VIP consultation packages
- Workshops and retreats
- Mastermind groups
- Other people's products and programs (earning commissions)
- Certification programs
- Membership clubs

This truly only touches the surface of all the possibilities open to you with an audience-based business. And our recent collective experience with Covid-19 highlighted the brilliance of it being on-line. Before we go on, I want to underscore the potential value your audience holds for you by grounding this concept in numbers.

Let's say that you were like my friend I introduced you to at the beginning of the chapter—a best-kept secret. You see clients one-on-one, generally about 10 a week. You don't have a list of potential clients you email; you've generated all your clients through word of mouth. Your max client load tends to be about 15 a week, and your hourly rate is $120, resulting in average monthly revenue of about $7,000. (If you are more of a product-based business owner, just do this exercise with your average monthly product revenue.)

You decide to reach beyond word-of-mouth referrals and build an online audience. Bit by bit, you are able to bring on more one-on-one clients, and your roster doubles. You're now averaging monthly revenue of $14,000—but you are working *so* hard. You see 30 clients every week. You hardly have time for anything outside of work.

The problem is, you've topped out your potential income earnings because you just can't take on any new clients. So you begin to offer group programs and courses to your consistently growing audience. You get to a place where you can count on at least 50 people from all around the world enrolling each time you offer it. Again, grounding this example in numbers, let's say you offer a month-long $500 program that takes three hours a week to deliver. Your revenue for that month—from that one program—is $25,000!

I mean, which would *you* prefer—30 hours for $14,000 or three hours for $25,000?!

That's the power of an audience. Now, to get 50 people enrolled, you're going to need a large enough online audience. How big depends on a number of factors, the biggest of them being: 1) Are you growing an audience of the right people, the ones who will need and buy your program? 2) Are you truly engaged with your audience so that when you offer your program, they jump to raise their hand? And 3) Are you using the best tool(s) to communicate regularly with your audience?

If your answer to those three questions is "No" or "I don't know" or "Maybe a little bit?"—no worries. That's what this book is for: to get you to a crystal clear *"Yes!"*

The Biggest Reason

Before we get into the nuts and bolts of that, I'd like to draw your attention to the "why" in your business—the truest reason to grow your audience. It's not just to earn more and work less. It's more important than numbers. And it's not just for you to break free and live the life you want for yourself.

Well, yes, it *is* for those reasons. We all want to make more money with the hours that we devote to our business. And we want to experience the freedom our business promises. But I'd like to propose a new perspective that places one thing above money, time, and freedom. Something that a well-oiled audience-driven business gives you.

Impact.

When you give up best-kept secret status, step into your biggest self, and affect the lives of the hundreds or thousands of people who join your audience—then you're doing something of enormous consequence. Want to see what that is? Answer these three questions:

1. What do you in your business help people do? Just two or three words. For example: get healthier, get out of debt, find jobs they love, be better parents, divorce amicably, look beautiful.

2. When people get this kind of help, what is the transformation that becomes possible for them? Some examples: they stop worrying, they no longer fear a heart attack, they

feel more confident, they're happier, their business revenues rise, they repair their marriage.

3. When they transform, who else does it affect and how? Think about your audience's spouse, parents, children, co-workers, community. When a person's life transforms, it *also* affects many others. How do *those people's* lives change?

When you consider these three questions, you'll see that you and your work matter greatly to the people who need them. You kick off a profound ripple effect of positive, forward-moving transformation. Whether you make beautiful jewelry, help people finally lose weight, provide hospice advice for dying pets, help displaced executives find new careers, create travel experiences, teach lawyers how to benefit from social media—*whatever it is*, your work matters to the people who want it.

So why would you want to play small, to deny your audience and their wider circle the gifts you bring? Why would you be okay remaining a best-kept secret?

I'll tell you exactly why in the next chapter. I've seen it; I've experienced it. And I know you have what it takes to get through it so you can start growing that audience, affecting their lives, and stepping into your own freedom.

ACTION MOMENT

1. What are four ways an audience can benefit your business?
2. What products or services do you see yourself offering your audience that you don't now?

Chapter 3
BREAKING FREE

"Scared is what you're feeling.
Brave is what you're doing."
—EMMA DONOGHUE

THERE'S ALWAYS A REASON. Or two, or ten.

I'm talking about the reasons *not* to step into visibility, *not* to build and nurture an engaged, buying audience—at least not yet. The reasons *not* to send emails—or *not* to send them more frequently. The reasons *not* to grow your audience larger or take it international.

At the bottom of this deep "well of reasons" is the same muck— whether you're just starting your business, whether you've played small for years and are ready to kick it up a notch, or whether your business is on the verge of explosive growth.

The muck?

Fear—in a variety of dark hues, from "concern" to "terror." More colorfully, we know it as "mental crap."

This mental crap is most likely responsible for more restriction (and less freedom) than anything else in your business, because

35

fearful energy pushes people away. Without dismantling this limiting force right up front, the danger is that you'll stay stuck, dreaming small and taking actions that don't really get you anywhere.

Fear tends to arise at predictable junctures in the life of a business owner:

- When you're doing something new or for the first time
- When you're acknowledging your expertise (suggesting you actually know something that others don't)
- When you're inviting attention (becoming more visible online)
- When you're asking people to pay you (claiming your value)
- When you've created something that you hope your audience will value (like a new book or program or freebie)
- When you're not confident or doubt yourself (imposter syndrome)
- When you compare yourself to others (and find yourself wanting)
- When you make a mistake, especially a very public one
- When someone criticizes you or your work
- When you have a lot riding on the success of your business (and people are depending on you to perform)

The bad news? When fear is holding you back or crushing your confidence, you are not free. All that freedom available to you when you develop an engaged audience-based business? Time freedom, location freedom, freedom to choose, creative freedom, financial freedom. It evaporates, leaving you frustrated and dispirited.

The good news—and it's *really* good news—is that fear usually pokes its head up (or opens its mouth to devour you!) *when you are ready to grow.*

Gretchen Kehan first heard the name of her business, Daughters Rising, like an intimate whisper in her ear that got louder. She was filled with awe and inspiration—followed only moments later by a flood of fear that washed over her entire body.

> *"I felt my heart racing and a weight on my chest as if I couldn't breathe. Whatever this fear was, it was deep in my body, in my blood, in my bones. This wave of fear was tethered to the very essence of my business."*

Gretchen first recognized the fear of judgment and how it held her back from building an audience, sharing her wisdom with them, and even crafting paid offers for them. Underneath the fear of judgment was the fear of being seen, of being rejected, of failure, and of being persecuted.

> *"Each time I would go to write a newsletter, instead of focusing on what I wanted to say, I would be overwhelmed by a sense of dread. What would they think? How would they react? Why am I even writing to them? In my head I envisioned eye rolls, talking behind my back, and laughter."*

When she began a deep dive into the fear, Gretchen realized that some part of her felt as if she was on trial with every word she wrote and each offer she made. She realized eventually that a part of herself was judging her decision to become an entrepreneur.

"The truth was, I was scared. Scared I would mess up. Scared I wouldn't be able to support my family. Scared of wasting time, money, and energy. Scared I wasn't good enough. Scared I would have to go back to a corporate world where I did not fit in. Scared I would be forced to leave my children and the flexibility that working for myself allowed for me as a mother and caregiver. Scared of failure."

It took her a full year for the wall of fear to crumble and for her to fully claim the name and launch DaughtersRising.net.

"I can now freely write the words that flow from my heart to the hearts of my readers without worrying what they may think. I can now create programs and craft offers, knowing they will be welcomed by those who feel called. I can celebrate unsubscribes knowing I choose not to wallow in pity or guilt but to celebrate and bless them, for it makes more space for those who are ready, willing, and able to be in the community I am co-creating."

Gretchen's experience is not at all unusual. Every business owner at some time or another experiences fear. Building an expert-based business is especially nerve-wracking because it involves so much of you. You don't get to hide behind products, because essentially, the product is you.

But your freedom is at stake if you don't step through the fear, like Gretchen did. And your impact is at stake. So let's go through this, shall we?

I find it helpful to examine fear by dividing it into three categories. It helps point the way to the best ways to dissolve the fear:

1. Vulnerability-based fears
2. Empathy-based fears
3. Logistics-based fears

Vulnerability-Based Fears

Being a business owner is one of the two biggest instigators of personal growth that I know of—the other one being parenting. If you've got confidence or worthiness issues in any area of your life, being in business is 100% certain to trigger those—in spades. And the visibility required to build an audience that will support and promote your business is one of the prime vulnerabilities.

Up to the surface will come all the self-doubt, the discomfort with being judged. Our childhood experiences that shaped us take on new life. The rejection, the failures, the criticism, the admonitions not to "show off." It all comes up! Turns out, playing small and remaining a best-kept secret isn't a choice; it's a *response* to these fears.

Of course, most of the time, we're not conscious of these dynamics. So we hold back, stay confused, run out of time, and so on—but what's *really* happening is we don't want to feel vulnerable.

See how many of these examples you can relate to:

❑ I don't like being a leader; there's too much pressure to perform.

❑ I feel stupid when I put myself out there online.

❑ People will laugh at me/ridicule me.

❑ People will think my _____ (product, service, program, freebie, etc.) is no good.

- ❑ People won't like me or my personality.
- ❑ People will say bad things about me.
- ❑ People will discover I'm a fraud and don't know what I'm talking about.
- ❑ Fear of making mistakes paralyzes me.
- ❑ I'm too private to develop a following.
- ❑ I don't have anything original or worthwhile to say.
- ❑ Being visible feels icky. I feel like I'm bragging.
- ❑ Compared to others, I'm pathetic/nothing/hopeless/dumb.

Yech! Just writing that list makes me feel a bit nauseous. It's toxic stuff. So what to do? I've worked with a mindset coach for years to help me work through the nasty voices in my head. They're not all gone. Just writing this book requires me to confront my gremlins constantly, sometimes multiple times an hour! But I have to say, they are significantly quieter and less lethal than they used to be.

A mindset coach is just one way to work through your vulnerability-based fears. Here are a few other really good tactics, which you can use on your own or in conjunction with a mindset coach.

Achievement Log

Keep a running list of all of your achievements, large and small. Write down anything that's gone right, anything you feel good about having accomplished (even if imperfectly) any time of day. These kinds of acknowledgments are like a lasting balm that you smooth over the wounds that lie beneath our vulnerability fears. It's helpful to look back through the days and months to see all that you have achieved. Include actions that are:

- Stretch-y (*Did my first Live on Facebook*)
- Practical (*Spent 2 hours researching my target market*)
- Congratulatory (*Made 3 sales today*)
- Emotional (*Made that presentation, even though I was so nervous*)

Comparisons

Don't compare yourself! I know, easier said than done. It's funny, though, how we only tend to compare ourselves unfavorably. The reality is that we are all on *our own* path, facing *our own* struggles and working with *our own* strengths. If you catch yourself comparing, find a strength. In fact, in addition to your Achievement Log, it's a great idea to also have a list of your specific strengths at the ready.

For example, as I was in the thick of writing this book, I noticed I had been comparing myself to a friend who is 10 years younger than me and has already retired. I was envying the way she had so easily added new, lucrative investment income streams over the past year. But when I took a step back, I realized that she has been talking about writing a book for three years, whereas I wrote this one in two months, from commitment to completion. *Our own* struggles, *our own* strengths…

Talk to "Them"

Talk to your fears and negative voices. Make them characters outside yourself that are really just trying to help in their own way. I always picture mine like the cartoon my son drew when he was 11 and I asked him to draw some "gremlins." The fears don't seem so fierce when I look at this depiction.

Business coach and consultant Ursula Jorch even named her beastie, a pink lizard she called Stella. Here's how she interacted with Stella.

"I started by patting her on the head to calm her down. That evolved into sitting her on my lap to comfort her. Eventually, she ended up on a beach chair wearing shades and sipping an umbrella drink and being pretty much unfazed by what I was doing."

Talk to Yourself

Affirmations can help break the spell of fear, too. Use some of these or create your own:

- My unique skills and talents can make a profound difference in the world.
- I'm proud of myself for even daring to try; many people won't even do that!

- My presence makes a difference in the world.
- I accept myself for who I am without fear of judgment and criticism from others.
- I easily connect with and am embraced by my audience.
- I replace all of the fear I feel with love and curiosity.
- I believe in myself.

Shift the Focus

When you feel afraid, nervous, or anxious, take the focus of attention off of yourself and put it onto the audience that you serve. It's so easy to get caught up in your fears and your anxieties, and you forget that you can fundamentally affect the lives of the people in your audience. Concentrate on the contribution that you're making to them, and you won't worry so much about your own flaws, failures, inconsistencies, and deficiencies.

Empathy-Based Fears

These seem like the "sweet" fears. After all, empathy is a good thing, right? And didn't I just say to shift the focus from yourself onto your audience? The reality is that these empathy-based fears are sneaky buggers because they disguise themselves as care and concern for others.

Some examples (tick the ones that tend to "get" you):

❑ I'll bother people if I'm in their inbox.

❑ People already get too much email.

❏ Everyone is inundated with information; I don't want to add to the glut.

❏ I don't want people to get distracted from my product by focusing on me.

❏ I prefer to highlight my clients or my team, not me.

❏ I don't want to turn off people who really need help.

❏ People don't need to spend *more* time on Facebook.

You may have already noticed the pattern. You're taking care of *everyone else's* feelings. You don't want them to feel bothered, burdened, overloaded, distracted, bereft, disappointed, and so on. But here's where the fallacy is: You're *assuming* that these will be their experience. You're assuming that your nurture emails will be unwelcome burdens instead of potentially transformative messages that are so helpful that people create a folder in their email program just for your emails! You're assuming that people don't want to know you, don't want you to shine your star brightly.

You'll make much more progress overcoming your fears if you stop sugarcoating them with faux empathy. "People already get too much email" is really much more likely to be about one or more of the vulnerability fears from above, which you're working on now…right?

When you own your purpose and your role as a conduit of transformation, you'll begin to see the content you use to attract and nurture your audience as flowers and diamonds—gifts that will delight and please the specific audience you're engaged with.

It reminds me of a favorite quote from the visionary modern dance choreographer Martha Graham that every entrepreneur should frame and hang near the computer. It's *that* important.

"There is a vitality, a life force, an energy, a quickening that is translated through you into action. And because there's only one of you in all of time, this expression is unique. If you block it, it will never exist through any other medium, and it will be lost. The world will not have it. It's not your business to determine how good it is, nor how valuable, nor how it compares with other expression. It is your business to keep it yours, clearly and directly, to keep the channel open. You do not even have to believe in yourself or your work. You have to keep yourself open and aware to the urges that motivate you. Keep the channel open."

Why You Matter

The best "fix" for this batch of fears is to return to the end of Chapter 2 and answer the questions that point to why you and your work matter:

1. What do you in your business help people do?
2. When people get this kind of help, what is the transformation that becomes possible for them?
3. When they transform, who else does it affect and how?

And there are two more questions you can ask at the end of that series:

4. When I am helping my audience to transform, and being well-rewarded for it, how do I feel, how do I change? For example: less stressed, more fulfilled, financially abundant, on fire.

45

5. When I transform in those ways, how does that affect the people in *my* life? How does their life change?

When you really internalize the rippling impact of which you would be *depriving* your audience, yourself, and many others, then you'll have all the reasons you need to keep moving through the fear of leading and nurturing the audience that needs *your* work.

Talk to Yourself Some More

Here are some affirmations that can help reset the dialogue between you and your fearful or critical internal critters:

- I am an inspiration to all of those around me.
- I honor the best parts of myself and share them with others.
- I give myself permission to shine.
- I don't have to be perfect; I just have to be me.
- I am an instrument of peace, hope, and joy to those in need of encouragement.
- I can make a difference.
- Positive energy flows through me to those I communicate with.
- My presence makes a difference in the world.

Logistics-Based Fears

Finally, we come to the bucket of fears that includes technology phobias and all manner of "I don't know how to do this!" freak-outs.

Ostensibly, these fears are the easiest to reconcile because doing so only requires learning a new skill, not dredging up early childhood sources of unworthiness. But they can be surprisingly stubborn!

For example, a woman I know had wanted for years to offer massage therapists online courses about business-building. She herself had a premier massage therapy clinic in Hawaii, and she had a lot to offer. She was a brilliant educator and writer, too, and had recently created several courses. It was the technology that stopped her. For years. How to get it online and deliver it, how to let people know about it, how to accept payments—she just couldn't wrap her mind around it. Yes, she could have hired a virtual assistant to do it or a consultant to walk her through the possibilities and help her make decisions. But in her mind, she had a tech phobia. Thinking about it made her feel emotionally dizzy, and that kept her from moving ahead.

Here are some of the logistics-based fears I've encountered while working with clients. Check any that have stopped you in the past:

- ❑ I don't know enough about my topic to put myself out there.
- ❑ I can't find the time to build an audience; I'm too busy.
- ❑ I don't know what to write.
- ❑ I don't know where things that I write should go.
- ❑ I start things, but won't be consistent.
- ❑ I can't figure out the technology (and, to be honest, I really don't want to).
- ❑ It's all too hard.

- ❏ I don't know which approach is best for me, so I do nothing.
- ❏ I don't know who to include in my audience or where to find them.

Flood the Zone

I live in northern California, where the Russian River floods its banks every now and again. Another definition of flooding is "arriving in overwhelming amounts or quantities." That's what we're after here: Take something that terrifies you and do *a lot* of it, especially in condensed periods of time. (Hat tip to Gemma Went.) The big idea here is that the more you do something that feels daunting, the easier it becomes. After not too long, it becomes old hat; the fear has dried up.

When I lived in Italy for half a year, everything was nerve-wracking at first. Trying out my limited Italian on the local barista, taking my first train to Rome from the little village I lived in, putting gas in my car, navigating the very-different grocery stores. But eventually I became almost completely desensitized to fear.

A steadier version of "Flood the Zone" with a gentler approach is to commit to doing something scary every day. And then acknowledge that action at the end of the day. When you do that, you build confidence in your ability to handle scary things, but you also become more and more desensitized to fear or failure. The only difference between flooding the zone and flowing with the river is the pace of breakthrough.

That's because action counteracts fear. Vincent Van Gogh said, "If you hear a voice within that says you cannot paint, then by all means, paint, and that voice will be silenced." And from Dale Carnegie: "Inaction breeds doubt and fear. Action breeds confidence and courage. If you want to conquer fear, do not sit at home and think about it. Go out and get busy."

Schedule Stuff

This is a tactic that really helps me bust through any resistance I have to big-profile projects, even if I curse it all the way through: Make it concrete. Internally, my gremlin is whining, "It's too hard. I don't know enough." And on and on. Externally, I give myself an unbreakable deadline.

I'm a champion procrastinator (because of all the underlying mental crap yammering on), and I knew I would finish this book only if I gave myself a tight deadline. So I committed to a publication date and asked colleagues to promote the book during a certain time period. The publishing company let me know what date I had to turn in the manuscript. Essentially, I had two months to write it, although it ended up being more like five weeks. Yikes! But without that compressed time period, the book might have never gotten done, or would've taken a whole year to write.

You can't pay much attention to gremlins when you're under deadline pressure, so eventually they leave you be.

Talk to Yourself Again

If affirmations work well for you, here are some good ones for these types of logistics-based fears:

- I am willing to try new things courageously.
- It gets easier. I just need to start.

- I easily meet and overcome challenges.
- I have a keen capacity to learn new skills that support my success.
- I am more than capable of bringing my dreams to life.
- I know that I can master anything if I do it enough times.
- I'm going to relax and have fun with this, no matter what the outcome may be.
- I grow in strength with every forward step I take.

You're here to serve people—with your products, your programs, your services. It's so easy to get caught up in fears and forget your value. All business is service in some form or another. You are here to serve, to fundamentally affect your audience, the people who want to hear from you.

So who are these people? Let's find out in the next chapter.

ACTION MOMENT

1. What is your biggest fear about growing an audience and developing a personal, profitable relationship with them?
2. What's the worst thing that could happen if that came true?
3. What could you tell yourself to break the spell of that fear and boost your confidence?

Chapter 4
DESTINATION: WHO

"No matter how good you are at your game, there will always be those who simply don't like what you do. Take heart, though, because your audience will love you for it."

—C.C. ADAMS

IMAGINE YOU'RE A 20-YEAR-OLD filling out an online dating form and you accidentally neglect to add the age range of your ideal match. Or a scientist shopping a research proposal to study only "germs." Or you're given a bow and arrow (and nothing else) and asked to "hit the right target."

What's going to happen?

You're either going to get a deluge of people you don't want (the 20-year-old), no responses at all (the scientist) because the organizations didn't see how your proposal applied to them, or you'll find yourself so paralyzed with uncertainty (the archer) about what you are supposed to be hitting that your arrow never leaves the bow.

The metaphors for identifying your audience are plentiful. And they all point to a central truth about your business: The more focused you are about who your audience is, the easier it is to attract the audience you want to serve.

Conversely, the less focused, the more likely you'll be to expend time and money working with the wrong audience, waiting for the right audience to come to you or just being frozen in uncertainty about what to do.

In addition, identifying a specific audience you serve helps you:

- Go deep in knowing and understanding their lives, their needs
- Create and offer products and services that your audience really demands
- Develop sales strategies focused on the needs and preferences of your ideal clients
- Write copy that speaks directly to the needs of the audience—in words they use
- Know the best marketing channels to use with your potential customers
- Effectively identify your competitors

So, yes, getting specific about who's in your audience is a foundational step. It's *also* one that many small business owners tiptoe over lightly or skip altogether. You may even already have been in business for years and think you know your target market. But until you take a trip with me in this chapter to excavate the many facts and facets of your audience, you may miss important details that could impact your business, positively and negatively.

The Value of Getting Specific

One of my clients, for example, had been working as a financial advisor for years. He knew his audience to be "retired couples in Texas." But once we got deeper into who they were, Chuck realized a number of things that completely shifted how he approached that audience. Just a few of his discoveries:

1. They were far more concerned about their adult children's financial well-being than their own.
2. They almost all played golf.
3. His client interactions were almost exclusively with the wives.

Knowing that prompted Chuck to offer two new services addressing the financial health of adult children of retirees, one for the retired couple and the other for those adult children. He adjusted all the copy on his website and in his emails to reflect a mostly female audience. And he started using golf as a metaphor in his consultations and throughout his online branding. The results? Business doubled!

By the time we finished, Chuck was able to describe his primary audience as "Female spouses of politically conservative retired couples in central Texas with investment capital of at least $500,000 who play golf several times a week and worry about the financial well-being of their adult children living on their own."

Do you see how different that is from "retired couples in Texas?" That's what this chapter will help *you* do.

Let me ask you something: What are you feeling right now?

- Eager?
- Confused?
- Resistant?

If you're feeling eager, great! Most business owners, however, fall somewhere between confused and resistant. *"But what I do can help everyone!"* you might say. Or *"I'm in no position to turn away any business right now."* So let me address a few things that might have you feeling averse to zeroing in on a specific audience.

It may be true that "every" adult in the world could use your help to better manage their time or reduce their stress or eat more healthfully. But where would you start to market to that entire universe of people? Where online would you find "every" adult? To successfully serve *any* audience, you cannot serve *every* audience.

You may be concerned that having a very specifically defined audience will shrink your business or cause you to turn people you'd like to work with away. Neither is true. The more specifically you define your audience and understand their needs, the more directly you can find them online and speak to them in a way that tells them you understand. Doing so expands, not shrinks, your opportunities. And defining your audience will never preclude you from working with someone you really want to, despite that person not precisely fitting your audience description. If you can and want to serve them, it's totally your choice.

If you're a person who values a very diverse work life, narrowly defining your audience does nothing to reduce diversity. If, for example, you were a health coach for female cancer patients in their 30s and 40s who are moms, there are many more topics on which you could work with your clients: grieving and regrets, finding joy in everything, parenting while ill, relationship issues, life purpose exploration, simplifying and/or organizing, and more.

And if you're reading this and thinking, "Yeah, got this," I want to encourage you to go deeper. There is likely more meat you can put on the skeleton of your audience description. If, for example, you were a weight loss specialist, you might say that you work with overweight women. But would you have the same conversations with women in their 20s who gained 10 pounds last year as you would with morbidly obese women in their 50s? No, of course not.

Or if you were a career coach, would the needs and terminology for a forest manager be the same as for a multinational corporate executive? Would the needs and concerns of a middle-aged restaurant worker about to be laid off be the same as those of a stay-at-home mom who's ready to reenter the workforce? No, of course not.

So let's get specific! You might want to grab a notebook right now to capture your thoughts as we go through the three primary categories of information you want to decide on for your audience: demographic, psychographic, and traits.

Demographic Identification

Demographic refers to facts that are external in nature and that will help shape where and how you reach your audience online. You need not include every type of data when identifying your audience. If, for example, religion has no bearing on the work you do with your clients, you do not need to specify. However, dig deep to see if perhaps you'd like to further describe your audience. Include as much detail as you can that is pertinent. The more, the better.

Here are the main types of demographic details you want to know about your audience:

- **Gender**: If neither specifically male nor female, indicate the approximate percentage of each.
- **Age range**: Don't make this too broad. Needs and messaging usually change with age.
- **Ethnicity**: If you don't currently target a particular race or ethnic group, consider whether you'd like to intentionally include more diversity in your audience.
- **Geographic locale**: State, region, country, globe? The good thing about an online audience is that it often *can* be global if you want it to be.
- **Religion**: Does including this info help or hinder your audience building?
- **Marital status**: Include if there is a commonality among your audience.
- **Family**: Young children? Teens? Intentionally childless? Aging parents live with?
- **Education level**: High school, doctorate candidate, MBA?
- **Work/profession**: Teacher, scientist, travel agent?
- **Career level**: Manager, principal, CEO?
- **Industry**: Healthcare, oil and gas, advertising?
- **Income range**: This helps you understand the purchasing power.
- **Relevant life experience**: New mom, cancer survivor, digital nomad?

Psychographic Identification

Psychographic information is all about the habits and preferences of the people you will be serving. It tries to get at how people think and what they aspire their life to be. The chief segments for you to consider are personality, lifestyle, social status, activities/interests, opinions, and attitudes.

Here are just a few good questions about your audience to try to answer. Come up with as many additional details as you can. The goal is to understand their inner experiences so that you can eventually speak directly to what pains them, what excites them, what motivates them. When you do this exercise and answer these questions, I recommend that you document the answers so that you can come back and refer to, or refine, them.

- What are they feeling in/about their lives?
- What are they wanting (personally, professionally)?
- What are they needing (personally, professionally)?
- What are they dreading (personally, professionally)?
- What are they struggling with (personally, professionally)?
- What keeps (or wakes) them up at night?
- What do they dream of?
- What do they aspire to?
- What brings them joy/inspiration/hope?
- What do they need to know to fix problems/reach their goals?
- When they get stressed about the topic you help with, what do they do?
- What's a typical day like?
- What brings them down?

- What lights them up?
- What do they fear about their future?
- What gets in the way of realizing their dreams/goals?

You might wonder how you can know all these details, all the answers to the questions. It's actually not hard; it just requires a little legwork. Just a few ways to get at psychographic information are:

- Interview individuals who fit your demographic details.
- Do a survey, online or offline, of those in your currently constituted audience.
- Browse books and magazines, online or offline, written for your audience.
- Pay attention to conversations in online forums likely to have large numbers of the people in your audience.
- Social media networks are a huge source of audience data, including demographics and interests.
- Your friend Google.

Traits and Characteristics

In this last segment of audience identification, you want to let your imagination soar. A person could match your demographic and psychographic details but not be right for you. So what are the qualities and characteristics of the people you'd love to interact with and work with that you haven't captured already?

Are they opinionated wisecrackers with a heart of gold? Earnest introverts who really want to do a thorough job? Do they laugh and cry easily or does adversity give them a tight-lipped determination?

Name all of the qualities you can think of that mean something to you, that make having them in your audience—and as your clients and students!—fun or easy or meaningful.

If you have already been in business a while, just describe two or three of your favorite clients/students. What did you like about them? About working with them? Make a list of all their attributes you enjoyed. Or, conversely, describe two or three of your customers from hell! Make a list here, too, of what drove you crazy and add *the opposite* to your list of desirable traits.

Skipping this step gives you less control over who comes into your business. When you're precise about who you want to join your audience and eventually become a client, you'll know how to tailor your marketing messages and audience-building efforts so that these are the people who come knocking on your door!

Now that you know so much about your audience, it's time to go out and find them! Continue on to Chapter 5 to discover how to do that.

ACTION MOMENT

Imagine a day in the life or the business of a typical person in your audience, and write about it. If you are in progress with your audience identification, just do a best guess. Even if you end up with a different audience, the experience will be valuable.

Chapter 5
DESTINATION: WHERE

"Potential audiences are real people found in real places."
—SUZANNE LACY

ONCE YOU KNOW *who* is in your audience, the next critical step in the process is to find them—online. Yes, you can speak
at local meetings and on the stages of national conferences. And
yes, you can network your patootie off in person. But we're talking
about cultivating an *online audience*, because that's what will set you
truly free! Here's how personal brand and style mentor Cyndy Porter
described it.

> *"I used to spend 70–80% of my time networking. I learned
> that these events and one-on-one conversations do help build
> connections, but they are very time consuming and the return
> on hours spent was very low. When I started speaking, being
> in the front of the room instead of the back, where I could make
> an offer from the stage, helped me tremendously. But the real*

growth in business occurred when I could find them, speak to them, and cultivate relationships online."

"Online," though, is a big place. (Massive understatement of the century!)

Good thing finding our online audience isn't just about searching for them "online." Rather, we can go to very specific online locations to find the people we want for our freedom following. Broadly speaking, these places are accessed through either social media platforms or other people's networks.

Below is a short description of the main ones being used by businesses today so you'll know what your options are. Then in the next chapter, we'll go over what to do once you find them.

Other People's Networks (OPN)

Collaboration for mutual benefit has been around since Stone Age hunters worked together to take down six-ton woolly mammoths. In the Digital Age, collaboration takes the form of multi-person online events, cross-promotion with colleagues, and taking advantage of other people's digital territory.

These activities all rely on the premise that people in your intended audience are already part of other people's communities or visitors to their digital territory. We'll talk about OPN *strategy* in another chapter; for now, here's a brief description of how you find "your people" in each type of activity.

Online Multi-Person Events

There are two main types of multi-person audience-building events (and dozens of permutations): a speaker series and a giveaway event. Typically, a host invites experts who serve the same type of audience either to be a speaker or to contribute a gift.

Experts participating in the event then let their own community know about it, collaboratively generating a large audience for the event. The event gives the experts the opportunity to present themselves to that audience and attract some of them back to their own community.

The key is to ensure that you participate with other experts who have a very similar audience to yours; otherwise, your message will be lost on the attendees to that event.

Cross-Promotions/Launches

This works to build audiences for beginners through super-seasoned online business owners via the communities of colleagues. Roughly speaking, cross-promotion refers to "I'll introduce you to my community if you'll introduce me to yours." Anytime you can get in front of people who are right for your audience—but haven't yet joined it—you have an opportunity to grow your audience.

Launches involve multiple colleagues introducing you to their communities and usually involve commissions for any sales generated; they sometimes lead to cross-promotion, but usually the commission takes care of any reciprocation implied in cross-promotion.

Podcasts

Podcast growth has really exploded over the past few years. Just three years ago, there were 500,000 podcasts available through Apple, and 44% of US residents older than 12 had listened to podcasts. As of January 2021, there are now 1,750,000 podcasts, and 55% of residents listen to them. So podcasts are huge and only growing in influence.

Being a guest on a podcast is a great way to make others aware of you and your business, for positioning you as a thought leader and for attracting listeners to be part of *your* audience. Hosting your own podcast multiplies those benefits, giving you the opportunity to build a listening audience that becomes part of your business audience.

Guest Blogging

Guest posting on the blogs of other individuals or organizations tells new audiences about you. Your audience grows when readers of those posts follow links back to your web page and choose to join your audience. It's a longtime strategy that still bears fruit—as long as the visitors to those blogs are folks you want in your audience.

Article Submission Sites

Article submission sites are content publishing sites that link people back to your website or to your social media accounts to (hopefully) join your audience. The goal is to get traffic that sticks without running paid ads. Some of the better-known submission sites are Medium.com, TinyBuddha.com, and EzineArticles.com.

Social Media

It's hard to believe, but 15 years ago, there was no Facebook and no Twitter. LinkedIn and YouTube had barely started. Pinterest and Instagram wouldn't come around for another half a decade. And new darlings to the scene like TikTok are only a few years old.

Fast forward to today and more than 4 billion people around the world now use social media each month, according to the *We Are Social Digital 2020 October Snapshot*. That's 53% of the entire world's population, and an average of nearly 2 million new users are joining them every day.

From the standpoint of an individual, the average user has eight social media accounts (even if they don't use every one of them each day) and is on social media an average of 2.5 hours each day.

So, without a doubt, social media is a good place to find—and research—your audience.

Just look at the monthly visits to the top most-visited platforms:

YouTube.com: 8.6 billion (global), 1.6 billion (US)
Facebook.com: 3.5 billion (global), 512 million (US)
Twitter.com: 2 billion (global), 535 million (US)
Instagram.com: 525 million (global), 96 million (US)
Pinterest.com: 420 million (global), 160 million (US)
LinkedIn.com: 200 million (global), 71 million (US)

While there are hundreds of different social media platforms, it's unlikely you'll need to focus on any but the above for your audience-building efforts. (Of course, that depends on your specific audience profile.) And no, you don't have to do all of them! More on that in Chapter 10.

Here's a brief rundown of these top platforms and an initial action or two you can take to get started finding your audience. Note that all statistics cited are from the above-mentioned *We Are Social Digital 2020 October Snapshot.*

Facebook

Facebook has been a dominant social media site in the world for some time. Despite some well-publicized rough critiques over the past few years, Facebook's prominence is not going away anytime soon, with 2.7 billion monthly active users clocking in. Users worldwide are 57% male and 43% female.

Posts (especially image-based posts), "stories," and videos are common ways to reach out. And Facebook groups are a huge tool for finding your audience, so it's good to know that more than half of Facebook users are members of five or more active groups. Of those group members, 98% of them feel a strong sense of "belonging" in those groups.

Find Your Audience (FYA) Action: Search for groups where your people might be. For example, if your audience is parents having their first child, try searching terms such as "parents of newborns" and "new parents." Review group policies; try to find ones that are not super-strict about mentioning your business. Join up to five of the most aligned groups (or more, if you can keep up with them).

Instagram

Instagram is one of the fastest-growing social networking platforms, with nearly 1.2 billion monthly active users. In 2020, it saw even stronger growth than Facebook. Although it does cater to a younger demographic, at least 30% of its users are 35–65-plus and that percentage continues to grow. Like Facebook, users are almost evenly split between males (49%) and females (51%).

Instagram is a highly visual platform, with users sharing primarily images and videos, though the livestreaming capabilities are becoming more commonplace.

FYA Action: Use Instagram's search engine (with words or hashtags) to look for accounts related to your topic and follow them. Begin liking, commenting, sharing posts and videos, and responding to their stories.

LinkedIn

LinkedIn is actually the oldest member of the top social media sites, having opened its virtual doors in 2002. And with currently 722 million members in 200 countries and regions around the world, LinkedIn is a well-established platform for professionals, as well as for business owners with a B2B audience.

It's a great place to expand your connections with colleagues—some of whom will have those OPNs talked about in the section above. Users can also share professional expertise through published blog posts that reside on the platform. Like Facebook, the male-female ratio for users is 57% male and 43% female.

FYA Action: Just like Facebook, search LinkedIn groups to get to your ideal audience. You can also create your own group and start posting your content to attract the right people. To interact with individuals who've accepted your connection request, use LinkedIn's internal messaging system to reach out and start a conversation.

Pinterest

If you think Pinterest is just for scrapbooking hobbyists or interior design ideas, that's not the case at all! Think of it more like a visual search engine tool, where you can show up for your ideal audience on themed image boards. Excitingly, Pinterest boards are evergreen for the most part, unlike Twitter and Facebook, where content is shared quickly, read quickly, and disappears quickly.

Monthly active users on the platform have grown rapidly in recent years to 442 million—more than Twitter now. Approximately 60% of users are female and most of those are mothers with children at home. Users are twice as likely to come from high-income households.

FYA Action: With Pinterest, it's easier and more effective to attract people than to search for them, although there is a search function and you can search for boards related to your topic and make a note of influencers. Pin to your boards frequently and consistently, and write keyword-rich descriptions for each. Follow and re-pin others' posts to get noticed.

YouTube

YouTube is the second most active social media site in the world, with an average of 2 billion monthly active users (30 million daily active users) watching videos an average of 40 minutes per viewing session. While there are some business models built exclusively around YouTube (think YouTube influencer), I'm including it here as a tool to find and attract your audience.

The YouTube audience is a bit more male than female, but together 77% of all US adults use it and all age groups are well represented in the user stats. If your audience is not based in North America, take comfort in the fact that 89% of YouTube users come from outside the United States.

FYA Action: Search for popular videos and channels in your niche and partake in the discussions going on there. Make video comments and reply to popular videos in your niche. Also, begin posting your own videos, and interact with commenters.

Twitter

The interesting thing about Twitter is that while it has 353 million monthly active and highly engaged users, nearly *triple* that amount visits the Twitter website each month. The belief is that a large portion of these nonuser visitors treat Twitter like a news website.

The demographic for Twitter users skews older than, say, Instagram, with 70% of users older than 25. And users are far more male (70%) than female. While follower counts can go into the millions (Barack Obama has the largest following at 128 million), the vast majority of Twitter users (96%) have fewer than 500 followers.

FYA Action: Follow the people who follow the brands you think your audience would like. Interact with those people through replies, mentions, or retweets (RTs) on their tweets, and follow back people who mention or RT you. Another way to find your audience here is surfing hashtags and checking relevant Twitter lists.

Clubhouse

Clubhouse is a live, drop-in, audio-based social networking platform that is *so* new, I normally wouldn't have included it in this book. But this app holds substantial potential to help you build an engaged community and grow your sphere of influence—and it is *blowing up*. Launched only in April 2020, Clubhouse already has 2 million weekly active users, as of mid-January 2021.

In a world over-saturated by screens, Clubhouse stands out because it is *only audio*, so users can be actively engaged while walking, driving, working out, and so on. Users join or create clubhouses and also topical "rooms." They either just listen, participate in, or host live discussions, with a focus on high-value conversations rather than produced content. And nothing is recorded. When the room ends, that conversion disappears forever.

FYA Action: As of this writing, the app is still in private beta, meaning that to join you'll need an existing member to invite you or "wave you through." It's worth finding a way to get in now so you can get the lay of the land and see how people are beginning to use it for business. All signs point to this platform being the *next big thing*. So when the app opens to the entire public, you'll have the edge.

So Now What?

You've described your ideal audience members and chosen the best places to find them online. What do you do with them when you've found them? You may be surprised at a simple six-word answer to that question. Read on; it's in the next chapter.

ACTION MOMENT

1. Name the two social media platform(s) on which your audience likely spends the most time.
2. List two podcasts where you might find your audience.

Chapter 6
DESTINATION: WHAT

"The best marketing strategy ever: CARE."
—GARY VAYNERCHUK

IMAGINE YOU AND I are at the same meeting. I walk up to you and introduce myself. The next thing out of my mouth is, "Would you marry me?"

How would you feel? Confused? Weirded out? Annoyed? Anything but *good*. Unfortunately, that's what someone new to your audience might feel if you were to jump into the wrong kind of action the minute you meet them.

The question of what to do once you've identified and found your audience is one that a lot of solopreneurs and small business owners get wrong—in several different ways. And that's putting a big boulder in the path of success and freedom. So let's talk first about what *not* to do before moving on to what *to do*—including perhaps the most important recommendation of this book.

What *Not* to Do

Sell

This equivalent of asking for marriage when you first meet someone is the biggest no-no of audience building! The goal is not to make money from them as soon as possible; do that and you're likely to lose them. No matter how or where you first meet your ideal audience member, the goal is to get to know each other first, to develop a relationship.

Request

Have you ever accepted a friend request on Facebook, or really any other social media platform, and gotten an immediate request to do something? *Get my free report, like my page, attend this event, fill out this survey.* Ick! Don't do that! You immediately risk being considered a "taker," not a "giver" in the relationship.

Lean on Lingo

Examine your multi-touch revenue attribution to determine your MQL process value. Do what? Whatever you write or say to your audience, make sure to avoid using industry jargon. You're an expert at what you do, so you know the verbiage and terminology. Your ideal client, however, is not the expert and may have no clue what you're saying. It's especially easy to fall into lingo if you've come out of corporate or institutional settings to start your business.

Impress

Yes, you want to make a good first impression with your potential audience. But that happens because of how you show up, not what you show off. When you show up authentically and confidently, you impress. When you show up consistently, you impress. When you show up and listen like you care, you impress. So don't worry about pushing the credentials or selling yourself. Show up like a real person.

Presume

"What you need is to take some time off and spend it on just you." Imagine you're a working mom now working from home because of the pandemic with young children *and* an elderly parent living with you—and someone you've just met tells you that. Imagine the side-eye you'd give! Exactly. Don't *tell* people what they need. *Listen* to what they need.

Trespass

This is a pet peeve of mine. Unless people have expressly given you permission, don't put them in your Facebook group or on your email list. There's no law or regulation against it. (SPAM laws actually don't prohibit adding people to your list without permission as long as you have an unsubscribe link in your emails.) But don't do it! It's annoying.

What *to* Do

Okay, tired of hearing "No, no, no?" It's a lot more fun to hear "Yes!" isn't it? So let's get into it. You've defined the audience you want to work with, you've found them online. And you know what *not* to do. Now what? The following actions and activities are not only proven to pull your audience into a deeper relationship with you—they're also enjoyable!

Lurk and Learn

We usually associate "lurking" with something creepy—lurking in the darkness or under the surface. In online terms, it means to read the postings in an Internet forum without actively contributing. To be honest, I just use it because it's more alliterative with "learn," and that's the part I really want you to focus on.

Whether you're browsing comments under a YouTube video, a Pinterest board, a Twitter thread, or wherever, this is a remarkable opportunity to tune into your audience that wasn't available before the advent of social media—and to tune in like a fly on the wall. If doing so requires that you join a group, select a few of them for each of the platform(s) you've chosen as best for your audience.

Spend some time doing this, without first engaging. Get a feel for the conversations taking place and for the tone. This will help when you engage later on. And take notes. Add to or refine the notes you've been keeping on your audience. You may discover that some of your initial understanding was incorrect.

By the way, I do recommend that you revisit this audience profile document at least annually. As you work more and more with your audience, it's a good idea to make sure you're up to date on who they are and why they're good for you and you for them. Also, if you discover a trend of difficult clients or unpleasant customers, revising your audience profile is the first place to start to course correct.

Engage in Conversations

I have a colleague named Mariah. It seems no matter which Facebook group I'm a member of, she's there and commenting in whatever conversations are taking place. Everyone knows her! Once a year, Mariah announces she's leading a retreat in Nepal, and every time, she's got loads of interest! Why? Because through her conversations, she's demonstrating that she cares, she's got the chops (her expertise area), she's on the ball.

I'm not saying everyone has to be like Mariah. I'm not. I prefer to lurk and learn, and then apply my learning in other ways. But for the right people, this kind of audience engagement is golden.

Be sure to respect the rules of the platform or group. Some don't allow promotion of any kind. But if it's a good group for you, stay and engage; authentic conversations will be plenty sufficient. There are ways to let people know what you do that are natural and do not go against prohibitions.

Ask Questions

Once you've established a consistent, engaged presence in the groups and platforms you're most active in, you can begin to lead and direct the conversations taking place. You can ask questions that elicit conversation—for example, on hot button topics or queries that provoke deep sharing. You can do a survey and share results. Ask for input on a new logo or book cover.

And please, be authentic. If you've been wondering something about your audience's experience, ask it. But don't feign curiosity solely to try to manufacture lots of comments. Your audience will always know if you're being real or not—even if they only know it unconsciously.

Invite Them to Your Email List

At the beginning of this chapter, I said I was going to make "the most important recommendation of this book." Well, this is it: *Your intention for just about every marketing activity you undertake should be to get people on your email list.*

It's one of the biggest mistakes small business owners make: not building and using an email list. Hear me: You can be a guest on 50 podcasts, you can speak on a dozen virtual speaker summits, you can spend big bucks on driving traffic to your website—and if you don't get people from those activities to an email list, the efforts become like steam, rising and disappearing in the air. How do you follow up with them? How do you build a relationship with them and make offers? They listen, and they're gone. They look around your site, and they're gone.

I remember the first time a colleague agreed to let me do a training for his list. It didn't even occur to me until a week after the presentation that I'd missed an opportunity to add people to my list. If I had had attendees register with me for the webinar, not with my colleague, I would have gotten their email address and permission to email them again. But hey, live and learn, right?

So think of your list-building like a treasure map with multiple roads, but each leading to the same riches: your email list.

But Why Email?

You may be thinking right now, "Why do I need an email list? I interact with my audience plenty on social media already. That's good enough." Or you might have heard somewhere that "Email is dead." In fact, both are untrue—and I'll show you why in a minute.

But first, let's back up for a definition in case you are brand new to online business. When I refer to your email list (or just "your list"), I'm referring to a collection of email addresses that you gather, with permission, and send marketing and promotional emails to on a regular basis. Some are clients; many are not yet clients but people interested in your work.

Over the years, there have been numerous pronouncements that email is dead. Never mind that those pronouncements usually accompany excitement about some shiny new technology. But somehow email keeps rising from the dead. Check out the venerable *Wall Street Journal*'s acknowledgment of this fact:

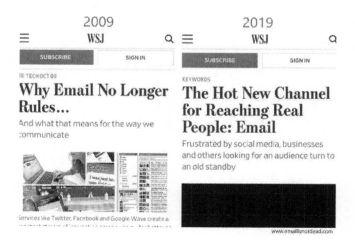

So if you hear that email isn't worth it, pay no attention! Rather, pay attention to the data:

- 95% of consumers check their email every day. —Data & Marketing Association (DMA), "Consumer Email Tracker 2020"
- Twice as many consumers prefer email for company contact over social media posts, text, or face-to-face. —Data & Marketing Association (DMA), "Consumer Email Tracker 2020"
- There are more than 4 billion email users, a figure predicted to grow to 4.5 billion by 2024—a growth of 3% yearly. —Radicati Group, "Email Statistics Report 2020-2024"
- 87% of business-to-business (B2B) marketers use email marketing for lead nurturing. —Content Marketing Institute (CMI), "2020 B2B Content Marketing Benchmarks, Budgets, and Trends"
- 78% of marketers have seen an increase in email engagement over the last 12 months —HubSpot, "State of Marketing" (2020)
- The worldwide market for email marketing will reach US $22 billion in 2025. Transparency Market Research, "Email Marketing Global Industry Analysis"

Bottom line is, email marketing works better than most activities, and it's only getting better. But let's bring this home to *you* and your audience. You're not a statistic. Here's why you need a list.

You Own Your List

You can't build your audience, nor your business, on rented property. Yet that's what so many are doing when they only build a social media audience. You may not know this, but tech companies own your social media connections. It's in the fine print. Your connections on LinkedIn and Pinterest? Not yours. Your friends and followers on Facebook and Instagram? Not yours. At any moment, you could lose your presence on any one of the social media platforms, and gone are all your people and all the work you put in to developing that following. Poof!

Mind you, it's not a common experience, but it's common enough that I know at least a dozen people it's happened to—sometimes for cause, sometimes by accident. And, you may remember that not too long ago, most of Donald Trump's social media accounts were canceled. From one second to the next, he lost 88 million followers on Twitter.

This is the biggest reason to get as many social media connections over to your email list as soon as you can. (We'll talk about how to do that in Chapter 8.) Your list is yours and no one else's. It is gold, your number one asset. When I sold a business a few years ago, we arrived on the price using a multiplier on the number of active subscribers to my email list, not on the value of the product, not even on sales. You take control of your business when you take care of your list.

Your Website Traffic Sticks Around

The most recent statistics indicate that 95% of the visitors who reach your website will never come back again. Isn't that sad? It's like your business has a hole in its bucket! You can plug that hole at least a little by giving those visitors a reason to stay in touch. Offer them a gift that you know your audience will value, and they'll give you an email address to add to your list. (See Chapter 8 for more on this.)

The bottom line is, you can try all kinds of fancy techniques to get people to swarm your website, but if you don't have any pollen, those bees will fly to someone else's audience.

Your Reach Is Greater and in Your Control

When the list is yours, you don't have to worry about other companies changing the rules on you. If, for example, Facebook wanted to encourage more ad purchases, they could decrease your reach with your fans. When your list is yours, these kinds of restrictions don't ever come into play. You land in their inboxes on the day and at the time you specify; you're not just a post that may reach 10% of your connections over the course of a week.

You Can Build a Relationship

Being in a person's inbox regularly with useful information means you're in a relationship. They've accepted you there (by virtue of having given you permission), and you prize the opportunity to be there. To go back to the marriage metaphor, when you send emails, it's like you're sending flowers and chocolates, showing you care. Remember, your audience doesn't want to do business with a stranger. That's why this process of you getting to know them by what they respond to— and them getting to know, like, and trust you—is so valuable.

You'll Make More Money

"Out of all the channels I tested as a marketer, email continually outperforms most of them. Not only does it have a high conversion rate, but as you build up your list you can continually monetize it by pitching multiple products." —Neil Patel, co-founder of KISSmetrics, CrazyEgg, and QuickSprout

What Neil says about email being more profitable than other marketing channels is true across most industries. For the most part, people want to be social on social media sites and do business on email.

But the part of Neil's quote that I want to draw your attention to is the second sentence, about how you can continue to monetize your list with new offerings. And, as we talked about in Chapter 2, the more engaged your list (whether it's a sizeable list or an intimate one), the more options you have to earn money without trading it for so many of your hours. It was by focusing on building and nurturing my email list that I moved into multiple six figures in my business. And you can, too, in your business.

You Can Establish Credibility Over Time

When you share your wisdom with your audience—and do it consistently—they'll come to know your expertise, and they'll admire how "on the ball" you are. Over time, both contribute to their perception of you as credible and capable.

You Stay "Top of Mind"

When you get your audience to your list and stay in their inbox regularly and consistently, your audience remembers who you are and what you're all about. They remember that you have something valuable to offer. Even if they don't open every email you send (not many will), they still see the subject line and *that you sent it*. So they're still reminded of you. Building a list and keeping in touch is the best safeguard against best-kept-secret status.

So we've gone carefully over what to do and what not to do once you identify and find your audience. And we've covered why it's so important to get them to your email list. It's all in service of your freedom, remember? When you get these pieces in place, you're that much closer to your ability to work from anywhere (location freedom), work the hours you choose (time freedom), call the shots in your work (freedom of choice), feel self-expressed and fulfilled (creative freedom), and be well rewarded for all your efforts (financial freedom). You're *free to*...create the life you want.

Now we want to turn to Part 2, "Free for..." This is where you'll discover how to use the concept of generosity to do the actual work of attracting and nurturing your ideal audience in service of your freedom. So, it's "free for" them that leads to your being "free to" have the life and business of your dreams.

ACTION MOMENT

List the seven reasons to build an email list for your audience.

PART 2

FREE FOR...

Chapter 7
THE ECONOMY
OF GENEROSITY

"We make a living by what we get,
but we make a life by what we give."
—WINSTON CHURCHILL

IN THE FOURTEENTH-CENTURY allegorical narrative poem *Piers Plowman*, by William Langland, there's a line that refers to taverners offering customers "a tast for nouht" (a taste for nothing) to entice them to drink at their pubs.

Benjamin T. Babbitt made a name for himself in the nineteenth century giving people free individual bars of soap, a novelty to the public at the time. So did William Wrigley Jr., except he gave free baking powder for purchases of soap. The baking powder became so popular, he began selling it and giving free packages of chewing gum, the product we now associate with the name Wrigley. He believed so strongly in the concept of "free" that he once mailed gum to every household in US phone directories!

And between 1894 and 1913, Coca-Cola gave one in nine Americans a free drink, leading to its easy status at the top of the cola industry. So it's clear that the practice of using free samples to interest potential customers has been around for centuries, and probably many thousands of years. (*"Here, have a little salt to try."*)

The Internet age gave a new twist to this very old idea, adding the exciting online potential to reach far more people today (without having to mail every US household sticks of gum!). An economy of generosity now forms the bedrock of every facet of marketing an audience-driven online business. And nowhere is that truer than in attracting and nurturing your freedom following—your audience of *just-right* potential clients.

It's a strategy that may seem counterintuitive at first—*GIVE my hard work, my hard-earned expertise away!?* But generosity is a practice that can catapult your audience-building and business far higher than you ever imagined and *more than* pay for itself.

In essence, "free" is like oxygen for your business, surrounding it and giving it life. And like oxygen, it's a powerful, elemental fire starter that helps a business grow voraciously. So that's our focus for Part 2 of this book: making things "free for" your audience.

"Free" Isn't a Trap or a Trick

Some perceive "free" as a trick or a trap. *"I don't want to trick people into subscribing to my email list,"* they worry. Done appropriately, though, done with intention and sincerity and your heart in the right place, the philosophy and practice of "free" draws the right people to you and your work.

You'll know when your heart is in the right place by how much you are looking to benefit the people in your audience, when you think of them and what they need more than you think about yourself. Just as the best relationships are about what you can give the other person, so, too, the best businesses concern themselves with what they can give their prospects and customers.

"(Givers) love to give," Bob Burg writes in *The Go-Giver*. "That's why they're attractive. Givers attract."

And look what that generosity attracts:

- Brand awareness
- Trust and credibility
- Loyalty
- Positive, enhanced reputation
- Attention to offers
- Traffic to your website
- Buzz around your campaigns
- Word-of-mouth referrals
- Invitations
- Audience growth
- Increased sales

Each of these contributes to the other side of the equation, where free leads to paid. As Zig Ziglar famously said, "If you are willing to do more than you are paid to do, eventually you will be paid to do more than you do."

The More You Give...

When you're deciding what and how much to give away, err on the side of more generous. Giving might sound good, but giving *a lot* might sound scary, confusing. Aren't we supposed to be in business to make money? Aren't we supposed to value our rates? So why would we give so much for free? It feels like a mixed message.

Buddhist teacher Sharon Salzberg reminds us that we have an initial impulse to be generous, but often talk ourselves out of it. But here's a proven fact that may help: *The more freely you give of your expertise, the more your audience trusts you know!*

A year ago, a colleague of mine was featured in an *Inc.* magazine article that illustrated this point. Before the pandemic, Shanda was leading two-day live events for up to 300 people three times a month. In those events, she says she gives two full days of "everything I know about business," holding nothing back. By the end of the events, 60% to 80% of the audience becomes her clients—because they trust that she's got far more where that came from.

If you think giving too much away means people won't ever pay you, that's just fear talking—the fear that no one will want to hire you. Focus on the dozen clients you'll attract by sharing tons of great information, not the one client you might lose because you shared too much information. Abundance is the name of the game. The more you give, the more you get.

As Burg puts it in *The Go-Giver*, "Your true worth is determined by how much more you give in value than you take in payment."

You Give It, You Own It

Let's say Person A and Person B have identical areas of expertise. They went to the same school, took the same classes, worked at the same company in the same position. They know the same stuff.

Person B writes a book on the topic and gives it away, creates free online trainings, covers the material in podcast interviews, speaks onstage about it, and more. Person A does none of those things, although, as we said, she knows the same stuff.

Who "owns" that topic? I'm not talking legally. Who becomes associated with that content that both of them know identically? Whose reputation is boosted? Who will people think of when they need help on that topic? Yes, Person B.

By giving away your content, you own it. You build your brand, your reputation, your visibility on that content. Ideal clients come to you. The more you put your stuff out there, the more you own those ideas in the mind of your audience, even if others are teaching similar topics.

Share from Your Life

In our Person A/Person B example, their knowledge and experience were identical. But, of course, that's not realistic. Even if our schooling and work experience were the same, our personal experience of anything is going to be ours alone. And that can be the most valuable content to share.

"The most valuable thing you have to give people is yourself. No matter what you think you're selling, what you're really offering is you," Burg writes in *The Go-Giver*.

As we'll discuss in Chapter 11, your relationship with your audience benefits strongly from sharing not only your expertise, but also from your personal life and wisdom. It helps people get to know you better, as a human, and leads to greater trust and loyalty. The two most opened, read, and responded to emails I have sent my audience over the years are the ones in which I wrote about taking my only child to college and about helping my dog of 15 years to die.

It's part of the "economy of generosity" to share of your expertise and your life. Moving on to the next chapter, we're going to ground that in specifics about how to put the philosophy of "free" into practice to *grow* your audience.

ACTION MOMENT

Why does "free" matter to your audience?

Chapter 8
GROW YOUR FREEDOM FOLLOWING

"The way you position yourself at the beginning of a relationship has a profound impact on where you end up."

—RON KARR

OKAY, WE'RE MAKING TRACKS! With a vision of your freedom and an understanding of the importance of an audience to that vision, you're clear on a few of your biggest fears about being visible. You're aligned with the philosophy of free, the economy of generosity. You know how to identify your desired audience, where to find them, and then what first actions to take when you find them.

In the next two chapters, we'll focus on two related but distinct approaches to audience. This chapter is about how to use "free" to *grow* your audience. Chapter 9 is about using "free" to *nurture and convert* that audience once they've joined you. Most of the containers are the same, but what you put in them is slightly different.

Before we start, I need to point out a common mistake made in both *growing* your list and *nurturing/converting* it, plus one big reminder. First, the reminder: As we discussed in Chapter 6, the bulk of your activities to grow your audience need to be *laser-focused* on getting people to your email list. *Email list*. Email list. Shall I say it once more? Email list!

Now for the mistake. Here's what tends to happen when solopreneurs start audience building: They make it all about themselves. *"I need to get myself out there so people can get to know me,"* is a common belief. So they spend their time creating a punchy, concise bio. They work on their 10-second "elevator pitch." They recite their credentials when introducing themselves on Facebook groups.

I don't want to make this wrong...but it is backward. It's inward-facing, when growing your freedom following needs to be outward-facing. By that, I mean in all your audience-growth planning and creation, your first and last thought needs to be always about *them*— the people in your audience. Yes, you will be positioning yourself and your expertise—your authority, some call it. But, as my journalism professors said all the time, you want to *show* them your expertise by how you address their needs, rather than *tell* them your expertise.

So as you begin the next step in your audience journey—creating the pollen-laden "flowers" that attract your people—keep in mind that it's all about *them*.

What do I mean by flowers? Well, remember that your intention is to create a relationship with the people who join your audience. Giving a gift is a great way to start a fruitful relationship. So, virtual flowers, if you will. Flowers with a "pollen" that the right people for *your* audience will find irresistible.

Yes, in our online world, we call these "opt-in freebies" and "lead magnets." But first of all...boring! More importantly, when you call them flowers, you'll most easily remember the true function of these gifts: to start a beautiful relationship with your audience.

Giving Flowers

In earlier chapters, you discovered where your audience hangs out online and began hanging out there yourself, learning more about their lives, their challenges, their concerns. Doing this is a great way to discover what kind of flowers will entice them. First you find them. Then you capture their attention with a flower they'll really want—enough to give you their email address.

Some of the opt-in flowers that still work well with audiences today are below. But don't forget that it's not really the *thing* they want; the *transformation* that the content provides is what they're after.

- Book
- Special report
- Webinar training
- Video training
- Mini e-course in series of emails
- Manifesto
- Assessment
- Audio recording (e.g., meditation)
- Checklist
- Discount coupon
- Challenge
- Bootcamp

Creating any of these is where you need to have faith that you can't give too much away. Twice I've written a full book and given it away. It's a *lot* of work. And I've welcomed tens of thousands of new perfect people to my audience with those books. That being said, some of the simplest opt-in flowers are often the most attractive. A checklist I created in two hours has attracted a steady stream of ideal clients for years.

Landing Page and ESP

Before you can start building your email list, your opt-in flower needs a place to live and a way for you to deliver it to the people who request them. The best place for it to live is on what's known as a "dedicated landing page." This is a page where you describe what people "get" out of the gift you're offering (aka the benefits) and ask them to join your list (opt-in) to get it. It may be a page on your website or it may be hosted by a third party that helps you create landing pages, such as Leadpages. And it's "dedicated" because there is only one gift per landing page and, aside from a sign-up form and a little bit of info about the gift and the potential transformation it provides, no other information.

To deliver the gift people are opting in to get, you need an email service provider (ESP). I'm not talking about Gmail, Yahoo, or the like or even yourname@yourwebsite.com; those are your personal email service providers. An ESP is more like a database that holds your email list(s) and lets you create emails to send to all (or segments) of your subscribers at once.

Ready, Set, Grow!

You've got your opt-in flower, your landing page, and your ESP all ready to go. So now let's look at all those places your audience hangs out to see what *specific actions* you need to take in those places to grow your audience. Before you hyperventilate, remember, you don't have to do *all* of these *right now*. You can add them on over time. You can pick and choose among them. You can mix and match. Don't let the quantity of ways to grow your audience paralyze you from doing any of them!

Online Multi-Person Events

If you're a speaker in a virtual speaker series, you'll either give a presentation or be interviewed by the host during your session. At some point, you will have an opportunity to offer one of your flowers. When you make the offer, be sure to summarize what listeners/viewers will "get" out of the free gift. Clarity on the next step in their career? A script to help make sales conversations more successful? A reward chart that nine out of 10 of your clients say has helped them lose weight?

If you're a contributor to a multi-person virtual giveaway event, you'll give away one of your flowers to everyone who wants it. You can also raffle off a bigger gift, such as spots in a program, for example.

In both cases—speaker series or giveaway—the people who like the scent of your flower will go to a page you have set up where they will enter their email address (and possibly a first name), thereby opting in to your email list.

If you're the host of either a speaker series or a giveaway event, your audience grows the most because you collect email addresses and introduce yourself to *everyone* who registers for the event. Plus, as the host, you establish some leadership in the area.

Both of these activities are where a lot of people start with their audience building. It's slow and steady, and you get to practice and refine your messaging.

Cross-Promotion/Launches

Typically, cross-promotions involve giving a free training to someone else's audience, rather than a simple download. When you offer the training, *you* put up the opt-in page and write the emails; your colleagues send the emails to their list. People interested in the training will opt in and join your audience.

Launches are like cross-promotions on steroids—take the above paragraph and multiply it by however many colleagues are emailing their list for you. You might want to start out small, with perhaps fewer than 10 launch partners. Once you're an old pro, you can have 30–50 partners emailing for you.

Podcasts

One of the fastest-growing marketing channels available today, podcasts offer two main ways you can grow your audience. Actually three, since listeners of a podcast are called an audience. But what we're talking about here are people who join your email list.

The first way is to be a guest. Like being a speaker on a virtual speaker series, the podcast's host will usually give you an opportunity to mention a web address. Rather than just give your website name, like jesusmaryjoseph.com, give a short URL that takes people to a page where they can opt in for one of your flowers.

The second way is to have your own podcast show, which gives you at least three different ways to build your email audience as you build your listening audience. At the end of each episode, invite people to subscribe, offering one of your gifts for doing so. Another way is by offering extra downloadable content related to the episode's topic. Think worksheets, resource lists, and the like. And finally, create a contest to raffle off a free product or service, such as a course or a VIP session.

Whether you're a guest or the host, you might also consider inviting people to a workshop or webinar on a topic you covered in the episode. Bottom line: lots of options with a podcast. That's one reason why they're so popular!

Guest Blogging

When you post on someone else's blog, be sure to include a link back to a "dedicated landing page" on your blog or website. This is a page where you describe what people "get" out of the gift you're offering (aka the benefits) and ask them to join your list (opt-in) to get it. Extra tip: Whether you guest blog or do your own, it's a good idea to have sign-up forms on your blog's header or footer, your blog's sidebar, at the end of each blog post, within the body of a blog post, and as a pop-up for new blog post visitors.

Article Submission Sites

Post original writing on the sites that you've chosen. Make sure your articles have plenty of beneficial keywords. And in the bio at the bottom of the article, include a link to the same kind of dedicated landing page as above, with one of your gifts and a sign-up form.

Facebook

When you join a Facebook group for purposes of building your audience and your email list, make sure it's one you're willing to engage with for the long haul. Post often and give lots of free help. Become a "regular" before you post anything about your business. You may need to ask the group's owner or moderator first, but if you've been a generous contributor to the group, chances are they'll say yes. Alternatively, create your own group. You'll have more leeway with group rules that way, but you still want to make lots of posts and give lots of free help for group members before inviting them to your landing page to get a gift from you.

Facebook Live, which allows you to create engaging content via video, can also help you grow your audience—as long as you give them a reason to go to your landing page and sign up. For example, do a short-and-sweet (and impactful) training, and then invite them to get a worksheet to help them take action on the training.

By the way, I don't recommend you use Facebook ads for growing your list unless you *really* know what you're doing or have very expert assistance. It can get expensive fast unless you make very strategic decisions.

Instagram

Instagram is slightly quirky for list-building, but still very powerful. The most common practice has you put a link to a dedicated landing page with your gift in the short bio area after the briefest bio possible. A free link-generating tool you might try for this is linkin.bio. And you get a greater percentage of people saying yes if the landing page specifically welcomes people from Instagram.

As with other social media, it pays to be highly active on Instagram, posting images, and liking and commenting on others' posts. Diversify the way you get content out using IGTV (longer videos), Reels (shorter videos), and Stories (24-hour disappearing content), and include clear calls-to-action to your landing pages. Some of your fans will want to be in more direct contact with you as a subscriber. The "Swipe Up" feature in Stories makes it super-quick and easy to get people to your landing page.

If you have a regular email newsletter with highly engaging material, you can give a "sneak peek" of that material to intrigue new subscribers. You can also run a contest, requiring opt-ins to be entered in the contest. Remember, as with all of your opt-in flowers, it's about showing people what value they'll get from it that makes the difference in your audience growth.

Finally, once you have built enough of your own Instagram followers, reach out to influencers in the space and develop an off-platform relationship to see how you might benefit each other.

LinkedIn

The key to LinkedIn success is getting connections, with a greater focus on the quality of the connection (how targeted they are to your audience) than the quantity. Start by sending connection requests and be sure to add a note to that request to personalize the invitation. Then use the internal chat system to reach out to start building a relationship with them.

Use the "Publications" sector to offer engaging articles and other content, always including a direct link to your landing page, along with a short description of the offer. LinkedIn Sales Navigator is an innovative and effective tool to help you grow your audience and gain recognition. Though it is a paid feature, it may be worth the expense because it enables users to conduct highly specific, custom, targeted searches with multiple filters.

Pinterest

With Pinterest, you don't actually need a large following to be able to drive consistent traffic to your dedicated landing page. If you'll remember from the description in Chapter 5, it's helpful to think of Pinterest as a search engine. The entire point of Pinterest is to attract people with audience-specific keyword-rich descriptions that accompany each Pin, and then invite them to click through to your website.

Like Instagram, Pinterest is all about images, but you can create image-based blog post Pins, pointing people to specific blog posts (where you include an opt-in message), as well as post images of your opt-in gift that take them to your landing page. Usefully, you can set your Opt-In Pins on Repeat. You can also share your Pins to relevant Pinterest boards, or even create a special board of your own just for your freebies.

YouTube

As the second largest search engine and third most visited site—in the world!—YouTube is a logical place to have a channel to help you build your audience. The same prescription applies to YouTube as to any other social media platform: Create content that will interest and engage your intended audience. With a loyal YouTube audience that enjoys your video content, the greater the likelihood of them signing up for your email list, to be in touch with you in one more way. And, as always, offer them an incentive (opt-in flowers!) for joining your email list.

YouTube has special tools that make it easy to add a call-to-action to sign up for your gift directly onto the videos you upload. "Cards" are an interactive element overlaid on top of your YouTube video. Annotations add interactivity by positioning a clickable text block on top of your video that links to your sign-up landing page. The annotations can look like a speech bubble, a title, a spotlight, a label, or a note, and you can physically point to it if you're in the video.

People find your YouTube video based on the description text you enter before uploading your video. Be sure to mention your gift and subscribe opportunity in this description. Also, be sure to add the link to your landing page to the End Card (aka End Screen or Endslate) that appears in the final 15–20 seconds of a video.

One other possibility is to use the "skippable" video ads function. These are videos of up to 30 seconds that run before the main video on some YouTube channels, using keyword-based bids for ad placement. These ads are watched by a surprising number of viewers.

Twitter

Twitter offers several tools to help you grow your audience. As with all other social media platforms, these will only work if you are *also* connecting with people and actually engaging—being social. You can always tweet out links to your opt-in gift. That's easy and simple, but could get boring. So diversify by using Twitter Cards, which include a multimedia element, such as images, videos, content previews, links to web pages, and so on. You can also use pinned tweets to send people to your landing page; these stay at the top of your page until you remove it, making it easy to put your opt-in flower invitation front and center for all visitors. And remember, three times as many people *visit* Twitter than are members.

Keep tabs on what is trending on Twitter; if your topic relates to what's currently being discussed, you can add that trending hashtag to your tweets to get them in front of more eyes. Other Twitter tools that can be used for list-building are Twitter Chats, which you can host to bring ideal audience members together to discuss specific topics and/or ask questions; Twitter Lists, which allow you to segment your followers, segment those *you* follow, and find new potential clients; Tweet Deck, which clues you into mentions of you on Twitter so that you can respond and engage; and Twitter Analytics, which helps you optimize the results of all the other tools.

Clubhouse

Because Clubhouse is so new, strategy and best practices are evolving. But it's already clear that it starts with joining "clubhouses" where your ideal audience gather (similar to Facebook groups). Participate in discussions and then host your own topics in "rooms" within that clubhouse.

When you go live with your own conversations, the members of that entire clubhouse receive a push notification so that they can tune in to your room. Users can check out your profile and follow you, too.

Another valuable use of Clubhouse is to develop business relationships with colleagues and potential collaborators.

Multiply the Action

I'll leave you with this last tip: Be sure to include links to your social media platforms on all your online territory. And if one of the social media platforms is your primary place of activity, be sure *that* link is all over the rest of your social networks.

Growing your audience is one of *the* most important business activities you will do. Period. So give it the attention it deserves. Reserve time each day for strategic actions on each of the platforms you use. And always remember your intention: email list. *Email list.* Email list!

The next most important business activity is nurturing that growing audience. Read on for why and how in the next chapter.

ACTION MOMENT

1. List one of the best "opt-in flowers" you've received over the years. (You can say this book, if you want—wink, wink.)
2. What did you like about it? How was it useful to you?

Chapter 9

NURTURE AND CONVERT YOUR FREEDOM FOLLOWING

"I've learned that people will forget what you said, people will forget what you did, but people will never forget how you made them feel."
—MAYA ANGELOU

I'LL NEVER FORGET THIS STORY....

Just a few years into her business, Donna Kozik was at a mastermind meeting in Las Vegas with her mentor, Adam Urbanski. As the meeting came to a close Friday afternoon, Adam announced a contest: who could make the most money over the weekend using strategies learned at the mastermind.

Though she was visiting with friends in Las Vegas that weekend, Donna's competitive spirit kicked in, and she created an audio postcard and sent a link to it to her list. She went off to hang with her friends for the rest of the weekend and watched the money roll in with glee.

Donna sold spots in her "Write a Book in a Weekend" program and "Book to 6-Figure Biz" individual coaching, and came in second place in the contest—a little more than $8,000 in just a day and a half. With only about 2,000 people on her email list.

But it wasn't just any ole email list—this was an audience Donna had focused on nurturing as she grew her business. She would think of a problem she was hearing from her people, and then write how a book would help that. She told stories of her authors and included pictures of them with their books. She emailed at least twice a week.

So when Donna sent her email on Friday afternoon with her audio message, her audience came through for her!

This is the power of nurturing in glorious action. Donna's audience didn't have to wonder if she knew her stuff, if they could trust her to deliver, or if they would enjoy working with her. *They already knew.* They knew that she understood them and what their struggles were and what drove their passion for their work. She saw them, and they knew that.

They knew this because Donna didn't stop engaging and interacting with them the minute they downloaded her opt-in gift. She sent regular emails generously filled with relevant, helpful information for her audience. And because of that, Donna's audience was already favorably predisposed to her and whatever she offered.

When I talk about the freedom available to you with an online audience-driven business, *this* is what makes that possible. This very act of nurturing your audience is what drives their conversion from potential client to actual, paying client.

A dozen years later, Donna is still one of the best nurturers I know. She conducts virtual study halls, she hosts get-it-done Facebook groups, she brings guest experts to speak on their areas of expertise, she gives away spots in compilation books she publishes, she does short Lunch and Learn virtual workshops, and she regularly sends great tips and resources. Plus she manages to do it while living nomadically, even spending a month with me and other solopreneurs in Prague via my other business, AdventurousLife.io.

"We live in such a wonderful time," Donna says, "when we have so many free or low-cost tools to help with this nurturing work. It's so important to create a sense of community by following up with your audience, letting them know you're there for them."

Donna says nurturing her audience directly contributes to the freedom she experiences as an online business owner. *Directly*. It positioned her as an expert with solutions to her audience's specific challenges. It established her as a credible voice and someone they could trust. Donna's consistent nurturing also got the attention of powerful allies, which grew her visibility even more and gave her colleagues to promote her work. And ultimately, it helped her grow her one-person business into a powerhouse training, coaching, and publishing company.

Nurturing Leads to Freedom

Interestingly, high-value nurturing helped me *shrink* my business.

In late 2015, I sat around a mastermind table with my own mentor and probably 20 high-powered business owners, many of them earning in the seven figures. One by one, we went around the table and talked about our goals for the coming year. And wow! There were some real reach-for-the-stars goals being voiced.

When my turn came, I could only whisper, with shame, "I just don't want to work."

I was embarrassed in that group of high achievers. I couldn't meet anyone's eyes. But I could say nothing more than what I whispered. *"I just don't want to work."*

Although my income had been in the mid-six-figures range for the past number of years, I felt utterly burnt out. I had a team of six people who worked with me, and the image I had in my mind was of someone whipping at my feet, yelling at me to dance faster and faster, and I was so tired of dancing.

Thankfully, my colleagues did not judge me but instead suggested that I take six months off and travel, which they all knew I loved to do. Which is what I did. I shrunk my team to one person working about five hours a week, cut my expenses about 90%, rented out my house, and set out on the road.

In January, I took three flights and a car trip to the tiny 50-person village of Laukvik on the edge of Norway to watch the northern lights. I don't think anything can ever surpass the magic of that experience. I spent time in Amsterdam, rented a car there, and drove to Bruges, Belgium, known as the Venice of the North—another bucket-list experience. A few months later, I hiked the ancient mountains of Crete.

I found that six months wasn't enough, so in the fall I wandered through Poland, Lithuania, Latvia, and Estonia, more places I'd been curious about. And in November, I had a stunningly memorable time in Moscow and St. Petersburg, Russia. I rounded out the year—a total of about nine months of travel—with a couple of months in Argentina and Uruguay.

And throughout my journeying, *I brought my audience along with me.*

Take a look at some of the subject lines for the emails I sent, nurturing my list and making easy-to-fulfill offers from time to time. It was fun to write about the travel and find the metaphor to connect the travel to business topics:

- Pics + OMG northern lights story!
- Message from Belgium + 2-DAY SALE!
- The AWFUL hike – and your business (Crete)
- Stories from the Road – Latvia + Poland
- Watching the elections from Russia
- Get me outta here – 20,000 to 700,000! (Uruguay)

So whereas Donna used her nurturing to grow her empire, I used nurturing to shrink my business for a while. The nurturing I had done for years and continued to do while traveling allowed me to earn the little bit of income I needed working very few hours. It also allowed me to have a business to come back to at the end of my sabbatical.

In both cases: *freedom!*

"Free" to Grow versus "Free" to Nurture

What does nurturing really mean in the context of an online business audience? The dictionary says nurturing means to care for and encourage the growth or development of; also to cherish, as in to cherish a hope, belief, or ambition. That's exactly what we do with our audience. We care for their business growth, or the growth of their relationship communication skills, or the development of healthy eating habits—whatever our topic area. And I believe that the most successful business owners do actually *cherish* the hopes and goals and ambitions of their audience.

Using the philosophy of FREE to nurture and convert your audience is slightly different from using it to attract new people to your list. You use FREE to *grow your list* primarily to catch the attention of your ideal people and show you understand. Using FREE to *nurture and convert* your audience is more about deepening and sustaining an ongoing relationship. If attracting your audience requires giving gifts and flowers, then nurturing your audience requires commitment to being in the relationship for the long haul. The rewards of that relationship multiply and come back to you in the form of increased visibility in your market, increased viability as a collaborative partner, and increased revenue for your business. Nurturing works because it:

- Increases your presence in the minds of your audience
- Makes you the one they remember when they're ready to buy
- Demonstrates your expertise, thus enhancing your credibility and trustworthiness
- Helps you "claim" thought leadership territory (become the go-to person for a particular topic area)
- Highlights to your audience how much you have to offer by how much you give
- Shows your audience how "on the ball" you are
- Establishes you as a colleague to connect with for mutually beneficial opportunities

And all of these result in increased sales of your programs, products, and services. Your nurturing makes sales.

The actual actions to take to nurture your audience essentially fall into two categories:

1. What to do with your email list
2. What to do on your social networks

Nurturing Your Email List

Nurturing by email means sending helpful free tips, resources, learning opportunities, and so on to your list. You can also send links to videos, audio postcards, inspiring poems or quotes, recipes, pet updates—you're only limited by your imagination, your time, and, most importantly, by what your audience wants from you.

Start your nurturing as soon as they opt in for one of your gifts. It's best to have a series of emails set up to go out automatically every few days for two to three weeks. These will highlight areas of learning from the gift they received and help you establish yourself as a beneficial presence in their inbox.

The easiest ways to ascertain the kind of info your audience wants from you is with a survey or in informal interviews. I also like to pay attention to what books and magazine articles are being written with my audience in mind. And always go back to the notes you took when you were identifying your audience. There will be a lot of clues in there about what topics they will respond to in your emails.

Frequency is a common question, and here's my advice: Send an email at least once a week, even better twice a week. It may seem like a lot, especially when you are just getting started. But any less than a week or two max, and people forget about you—an unfortunate fact, but true. There are resources to help you with content creation so you don't have to spend all your time writing helpful articles (Ready2GoArticles.com is one of them).

One last tip on your nurturing emails is to spend time with your subject lines. They are the biggest drivers of whether your audience will open your emails. You'll still spark awareness just by landing in someone's inbox, but it's even better when they open and consume the email.

The best subject lines are short, clear, and intriguing. And if there is time-sensitivity in the email, be sure the urgency is in the subject line.

Nurturing on Social Media

It's all in the name—*social* media. Nurturing on the social media platforms included in this book mostly boils down to interacting frequently with the connections you are making. On Facebook, your nurturing works best in groups, engaging with your audience and offering your free help, tips, and the like. On YouTube, keep posting helpful videos, and then interact with the commenters. Offer engaging articles on LinkedIn, and curate your images on Pinterest and Instagram with an eye for your audience's interests and preferences. Connect, connect, connect. (And don't forget: Your ultimate social media goal is to get your audience onto your email list!)

Remember, It's About *Them*

Get in the mental habit before you do any nurturing—writing an email, posting on social media, and so on—of remembering your audience and their specific challenges, needs, experiences. Soon enough, you'll be able to do that without consciously reminding yourself. Until then, try putting a stickie on your laptop or desk to keep that front and center as you nurture your audience. And thereby nurture your freedom.

If all of this about attracting and nurturing your audience sounds like a lot of work—it is! But don't worry, I've got some strategies for you in the next chapter to keep the overwhelm at bay and the stuck areas free flowing.

ACTION MOMENT

How does nurturing your audience lead to freedom? For you and for them?

PART 3
FREE FROM...

Chapter 10
IT'S YOUR CHOICE

"Promise me you will not spend so much time treading water and trying to keep your head above the waves that you forget, truly forget, how much you have always loved to swim."

—TYLER KNOTT GREGSON

SPEAKER SUMMITS, podcasts, Facebook, opt-in gifts, nurturing, Instagram, cross-promoting, giveaways, YouTube, articles, webinars—and on and on.

Feeling overwhelmed yet? I do, just writing it!

Here's the good news: *You don't have to do it all.* Remember freedom of choice? Yeah, you get to choose what's right for you. You can go slow in your audience-building; you can go fast. You can build an empire; you can create a simple freedom for yourself.

And so we come to Part 3 of this book. In Part 1 ("Free to…"), we explored how building and nurturing an online audience creates freedom in your life and business. In Part 2 ("Free for…"), we reviewed how to use the philosophy of FREE and the economy of generosity to bring your audience to you and nurture the relationship so that they become clients and customers. Now, in Part 3 ("Free from…"), we look at how to stay *free from* struggle in your audience work, and how building your audience actually *protects* you from the vicissitudes of business and life.

In Chapter 10, we'll cover how to support your audience-building efforts so that you can stay in action and out of overwhelm. We'll also take a closer look at social media to see which platforms make the most sense for you to do. There is value in simplicity and focusing on your strengths. We'll talk about that.

Setting Up for Freedom and Flow

There's one thing that derails freedom—your freedom—more than almost anything. It's overwhelm. As a solopreneur or small business owner, it's *easy* to get overwhelmed. So much to do, so many hats to wear, so many decisions to make—and often all by yourself.

Unfortunately, what usually gets ditched when business gets overwhelming is audience building and nurturing. These activities seem "ditchable" because they're seen as "soft" marketing and not *directly* responsible for bringing home the bacon. They're easier to sacrifice on the altar of too-much-to-do, especially if you haven't developed plans or habits for your "audience work."

That is *so* counterproductive to the freedom you are creating for yourself. When you let your audience activities go stagnant, you are turning off the real engine of your business. Your business may do alright if it's coasting, like a car down a San Francisco hill. But when that road flattens or, heaven forbid, starts going up another hill, you want that engine to be humming.

Following are three practices that make all the difference to getting and staying in action with your audience-building and

-nurturing activities—and doing so with delight and momentum, not overwhelm.

Recognizing Resistance

When you find yourself putting off your audience work week after week, month after month, you might be thinking that it's because you just don't have enough hours in a day. Or you might be saying to yourself, "I'll get to it tomorrow; today just didn't work." Day after day.

Steven Pressfield, author of several books including *The War of Art*, says it's not the lack of hours or that "today" just didn't work. He calls it resistance, those inner roadblocks that keep us from fulfilling our potential.

"Procrastination is the most common manifestation of resistance because it's the easiest to rationalize," he writes. "We don't tell ourselves, 'I'm never going to write my symphony.' Instead, we say, 'I *am* going to write my symphony; I'm just going to start tomorrow.'"

So it's resistance that is the culprit. Underlying that resistance are going to be some of those fears articulated back in Chapter 3 and usually a healthy dose of "If I don't do this perfectly..." mental chatter. Realize there is no such thing as perfection. Get used to things not being done perfectly. Get used to making mistakes. When you build a solid relationship with your audience, they'll easily forgive you!

Remember to take the focus off yourself. Keep it trained on your audience—on helping *them* transform their challenges. Take yourself out of the process. Allow yourself to be motivated by love rather than fear. Yes, love for your audience. Normally I sign off on all my emails "To your brilliant success." But sometimes I feel the love for my audience so strongly that I sign off with a more intimate "Much love."

On a more practical level, understanding your "style" of working can also help with resistance. Some people work best with routine. Others work best with a more project-based approach, getting a bunch of writing and other audience work done in one go versus doing something on the same day every week.

If you're a routine-oriented person, designate one day a week that is "Audience Day" for the bigger tasks and 30 to 60 minutes daily for the rest. If you're a project person, try doing a monthly or quarterly "Audience Retreat." In one weekend, you should be able to write a *lot* of content. If you get distracted in your normal home or office surroundings, go somewhere, even if you just check into a local hotel room where there's nothing to divert your attention. One of my favorite retreats was to Lake Tahoe in California. There was something about the beauty of the outdoors there that inspired my writing.

Another practice that can help lower resistance is to keep an idea journal so you're not sitting down with a blank screen and nothing decided to write about. If, like me, you get your best ideas in the car, use your phone to record them. If you don't capture your ideas, they can easily fly away as if you never had them.

Planning

"The most pernicious aspect of procrastination is that it can become a habit," Pressfield says.

Planning and scheduling prevent procrastination. When you know what you're going to write about and when, what offers you're going to make and when, what list-building activities you'll be under-taking and when—when you know all that and specifically when you're going to do it, procrastination just doesn't get as much of a stronghold.

Create an annual calendar for your audience work. Do this as far in advance as you can (a quarter, six months, a year). Your income-earning activities get first priority in your calendar, so start by entering the dates of paid promotional campaigns. Next, calendar your list-building activities so that you're intentional and consistent. Too often, business owners look back at the end of the year and real-ize that their list-building didn't really happen that year—again. The only way to make sure it does is to plan for it.

Next, add dates and topics for your nurture content. You can synchronize the topics with those of your campaigns so that your ar-ticles and social media support the topic of the paid programs you're offering. You can even create a production calendar, where you give a date to all pieces of the production process, from start to finish, for the entire year. When will you write your nurture emails, your social media posts? When will you edit and proofread or send to the person who will do that? Load stuff up into your email service provider or social network?

When you lay this out for the whole year, and write the tasks in your calendar, you don't have to "reinvent the wheel" each month or every time a deadline looms. You'll know the drill, the order, and it's all laid out there in your calendar for you. When you have a plan, you can act on that plan. You can carry out and implement that plan. When you have *no* plan, your vision is fuzzy and everything feels stressful.

Getting Help

It's easy to fall prey to the dreaded "Lone Ranger Syndrome" when you're growing and nurturing your audience. That's the malady that makes you say things like, "It's just better if I do it myself," and "I can't afford to outsource," and "It'll have to wait until I can get to it." Instead, you stay up all hours. You struggle with new software programs, new skill sets. You push harder and harder just to get it all done. And that's the problem: It's not getting done.

Of course, there are tasks that appropriately belong to you and you alone—but probably far fewer than you might imagine. If you're that Lone Ranger wondering how to know when it's time to get off your horse and get some help, these questions can help give you clarity.

- How important is this task to the well-being of my business? To the growth of my business?
- Do I really need to do this myself? Why?
- Do I really have the skills I need to do a good job at this task?
- Do I really *want* to learn the skills I'll need to do this task well?
- How much time would I realistically spend completing this task at a standard that I would like?
- Multiply that realistic time estimate by your hourly rate, and ask again, "Is it really cost-effective for me to do this task?"
- What am I afraid of if I let someone else do this task?
- Is there some portion of a task that I can let go of, if not the entire thing?

- What else could I be doing for my business with the time I've saved by outsourcing a task?
- What else could I be doing for myself with the time I've saved? How does taking care of myself that way help my business?

When I was a couple of years into my business, I was sitting at my desk, rummaging through backs of envelopes for someone's phone number. I didn't think I could afford to hire an assistant, but in that moment of frustration, I realized that my business would implode if I didn't get help. Best decision ever. When you step out to get support, even when you don't think you can afford it, the increased earnings made possible when you're *free from* the tyranny of having to do everything will more than cover the cost of your assistance.

And I have to say, having support feels divine! When I was on my sabbatical, I took care of whatever small amounts of work needed to be done, and it was no big deal. It was actually kind of enjoyable, after having taken care of a team of six for so long. Once I came back, though, it took me a couple of years before I realized that I was doing that Lone Ranger thing again. I gradually increased my support, and in 2020, I welcomed more of it than ever before. Delicious!

Choosing Your Social Networks

I have a confession to make. I *barely* use social media for building or nurturing my audience. You may find that odd or confusing, since I've taught you about it in this book. I'm not against it. I know what to do and what works. What little I've done has gotten me decent results. I just don't enjoy using it for business all that much.

I know, I know—there are lots of things we do in our businesses that aren't always enjoyable. (Bookkeeping, anyone?) I do believe in stretching and growing, and have done plenty of it in business. I acknowledge that it's possible to change, and who knows, maybe I will someday fall in love with social media. I also acknowledge that perhaps my business would be bigger if I focused more on social media.

It's just not my gig.

I make the rare video here and there. I hosted a Facebook challenge once. I post from time to time in my Adventurous Life Facebook group. My Instagram account has one photo; I just use it to follow my son and his wife. I'm checking out Clubhouse. That's about it.

And yet...

And yet, I've been making multiple six figures for years. I figured out what works for me. I don't fret about missing out. I'm *free from* any guilt or self-criticism about my decision. It's my choice, and it's working.

You get to decide, too! I know it may sound heretical, but I'm a firm believer that you get to decide how you want to grow and nurture your audience. If those ways work well for you in attracting your followers, do those! Don't let any "shoulds" you might hear feel oppressive. You are *free* to choose.

To help you decide what suits you best, it's helpful to look at the various platforms as personalities. The key is to find the right one(s) for you, and then commit to use it frequently and expertly.

The Maryland-based marketing agency Ironmark put together an amusing and insightful personality description for each of the main social networks. Based on those, here's a look at where you best fit:

Facebook—The "No-Clique" Type

Facebook is like the person named Class Favorite in high school who knows and is liked by everyone. People of all ages, income levels, religions, and genders are here, so it's a good general playground.

Instagram—The Young and Hip Type

If you're young or young at heart, if you're clued in to pop culture, if you don't shy away from selfies or you just love photos, Instagram may be the one for you. Also if you have a physical product–based company.

LinkedIn—The Business Professional Type

Are you more statistical than satirical? A little more "business-forward" perhaps? Someone who loves connecting with large numbers of people, and even connecting them with other people? This is your jam.

Pinterest—The Inspirational and Clever Type

Remember, this is the most search-engine-like of all the platforms. Can you inspire through images and photos? Then this may be the place to generate leads for you.

YouTube—The Unique and Personable Type

It's all about the video here. If you like being on camera and have charisma—or if your product/service is highly visual and unique—YouTube could be brilliant for you.

Twitter—The Quirky and Informed Type

Is witty repartee your thing? Are you pretty up to date with current events? Do people say you have quirky, clever "takes" on a topic? If yes to these, then Twitter is for you!

Play to Your Strengths

When you select the social platforms that you most align with, you're practicing a concept that would be good to call out here: focusing on your strengths rather than your weaknesses. We humans tend to think that our weaknesses matter more in holding us back than our strengths matter in advancing us.

To be *free from* feeling overloaded, obligated, or oppressed in your audience building and nurturing, stop doing battle with what you don't do well. The authors who first brought this breakthrough theory to our attention 20 years ago, Marcus Buckingham and Donald Clifton, say that, yes, you can work to add skills and knowledge to increase your performance, but unless you are building upon one of your innate talents, your efforts may produce small results, but not dramatic improvement.

"Unless you have the necessary talent, your improvements will be modest," they write in *Now, Discover Your Strengths*. "You will be

CHAPTER 10: IT'S *YOUR* CHOICE

diverting most of your energy toward damage control and very little toward real development."

So when it comes to growing and nurturing your audience, what are your strengths? Mine are writing and speaking improvisationally with others about the two topics of my businesses: audience and traveling with your business. That's why I focus most of my marketing on sending emails and am always ready to go for a podcast or live Q&A session.

What about you? Review the plethora of tactics we've gone over so far in this book for adding to your audience. Which ones jump out at you? Perhaps you'll need to explore a bit before you find your activities and channels. You may also need to explore finding your voice with your following. One way to do that is by getting personal with your audience. We'll consider that and other ways to get your audience to stick around in the next chapter.

ACTION MOMENT

1. When you put things off, what's the outcome you are trying to prevent?
2. What's your best way to snap yourself out of overwhelm?

Chapter 11
FINDING YOUR VOICE

*"Nothing influences people more
than a recommendation from a trusted friend."*
—MARK ZUCKERBERG

WHEN LESLEY NASE moved away from her community of many years, she left behind like-minded friends, spiritual support—and her old way of doing business. Lesley helped people and their pets bond on a deeper level through intuition, animal communication, and healing. She is also a shamanic practitioner and psychic medium, and clients had always come to her through word-of-mouth referrals, workshops, and speaking events.

To help her move her business online, Lesley went all in with an organization and one individual in particular. She learned about keywords and phrases, marketing tools, and positioning. She had them rebrand and overhaul her website, create a Facebook page, and put a signature course online.

She was doing all the "parts" she thought she was supposed to, but something felt off.

"I was so caught up in following the expert's advice I lost sight of myself and my desire to be of service."

The expert told her she was too "woo-woo," didn't know how to write copy, should build her email list fast with Facebook ads (for a high monthly investment), and should push to sell right off the bat in her welcome emails with scare tactics like "If you don't..." and "I'm surprised you didn't...."

"It got to the point that every time I got off the phone with this person I was in tears. He was coming from an old-school, used-car salesperson viewpoint, and it just didn't feel like me."

Her results were dismal; he told her she wasn't trying hard enough. (What an atrocious example of how *not* to help your clients!)

In this environment, Lesley found she was so fearful of doing things wrong that she hardly ever wrote emails to her email list. An old gremlin came back to haunt her. "You can't write because you're dyslexic," it told her ruthlessly.

After attending one of my bootcamps in 2020, Lesley vowed to write one nurturing email a week no matter what. It was scary at first, and she would often find herself struggling all week with the email, not sending it out until Friday. But she kept her vow and sent a nurture email every week.

"After about six weeks, I was getting more people opening my emails, along with people unsubscribing. It felt good to have both those who were interested and those who were not my

ideal clients showing themselves. It also felt good to get back to a sense of joy and service."

Starting at Thanksgiving, Lesley began telling personal animal stories related to the work she does. Her writing flowed even more, and she found that she actually loved telling these stories. Three weeks later, she began receiving bookings from people wanting to talk about hiring her—something she describes as a *huge* win for her. It set her up in 2021 for the kind of authentic relating and natural sales that she was craving.

Writing from Your Heart

Lesley's story is surprisingly common. By writing to her list every week, Lesley *developed* her voice. She didn't start out knowing exactly what her message was. She'd never delved into her point of view, those opinions that flavor your approach to your topic. She grew into it.

In the beginning, it was like pulling teeth, but she broke through the resistance and negative voices at least enough to get her emails out by Friday. Her readers started giving her feedback by increasingly opening her emails. Then when she started sharing her personal experiences—sharing from her heart—the transformation was complete. Her audience was bonding with her, valuing her work, wanting more from her.

And this happens *through* writing, not because of it. It's the *practice* of writing that draws your audience to you and makes them stick around. And yes, like in Lesley's case, people will unsubscribe. This is good, because the ones who stay are the further refinement of your audience. Some people get freaked out about unsubscribes. But hear this: You're not in the business of avoiding unsubscribes. You're in the business of connecting with the right people for you, and those unsubscribes help you do that.

Why Your Audience Sticks Around

Let's review. Your audience sticks around because:

- They like you.
- They value you.
- They trust you.
- They're interested in your work.
- They're interested in you.

And one of the best ways to feed all five of those is to share from your life and experience, to be yourself. Not who you think you're supposed to be. (For example, *I'm supposed to be nice and not offend anyone.*) Not who you think *they*, your audience, wants you to be. Not faking it. But showing them that, in addition to being smart in your area, you're also real, you're human. And you do that by getting personal in your communications. So let's explore that—what to do and what not to do.

Your Stories Matter

The power of stories is huge because we are *wired* for story. Think of the oral traditions handed down for centuries, maybe even millennia: mythologies around the world, theater, clowns, books, movies. It's all about our experience as humans, and we are absolutely magnetized to it. We love hearing about other people's lives, their foibles and failures, triumphs and tragedies, messes and miracles. It attracts attention and interest and engagement.

Your stories also have value. They educate, they inspire, they model what's possible, they warn and caution, they invite introspection on the part of the reader, they prompt aha's and growth. I don't care if you have a subscriber base that is C-suite executives; they're still human and they will still respond to the personal.

There are so many ways to include personal info. I'll share a few to give you a flavor.

Behind-the-scenes. One of my students had a section in her newsletter called "Husband of the Artist," and in that section, yes, her husband "dished" on his wife's art and painting process.

Quirky factoids. A law firm would share videos of its lawyers answering questions, such as "What superhero would you be and why?" and "If you weren't an attorney, what would you be?"

Personal journeys. A weight-loss coach I know wrote powerfully about her *own* journey through weight loss and how self-love helped her release her extra, protective weight.

Children. All kinds of parenting experiences are good topics, even if your business has nothing to do with parenting and even if you don't use the stories to jump off into lessons for your audience. I once included an audio of my son singing in his high school musical. (That's when I discovered he had a truly amazing voice!)

Parents. Once I surprised my mom on Mother's Day by flying to Texas and pretending to be a waitress where she and my siblings were having brunch. She didn't recognize me even when she gave me her drink order! I learned that is called "perceptual blindness" and wrote an article about how solopreneurs can be perceptually blind in their businesses.

Pets. Pets are heart-warmers for every reader. Think getting a new one, caring for a sick one, death of one, funny stories, an experience with your pet to illustrate a teaching point, and so on. Sometimes all you need to do is include a photo, like the one of my dog giving me a big, sloppy kiss upon my return from a few months in Italy.

Travel experiences. This is my personal favorite. I love finding the business metaphor for funny or inspirational travel experiences. Like the time I got locked in a closed department store in Rome at night. Or the ballet-dancing nuns from around the world serving dinner (it's true!). My people love to travel, and if they can't be there with me, they want to travel vicariously through me.

Hobbies or new things you're learning. I wrote a lot of business articles about learning tango when I was in Argentina for a couple of months. That experience actually inspired one of my readers to do the same, and she eventually moved to Buenos Aires and studies with my tango teacher to this day.

A personal milestone or accomplishment. Did your business just turn 15? Tell a story about the early days. Just ran your first marathon? Use it to write to your audience about perseverance and determination.

Something that moved you. The stunning acrobatic dance by a one-armed ballerina. A Ted Talk. A letter you received from a client. Discovering you have a half-sister.

Getting Personal Dos and Don'ts

As to how personal to get and how much to reveal, that's something you'll have to feel out for yourself; it always depends on you and your audience. But I have seen some people overshare—to their detriment. It may work for *some* individuals to give blow-by-blows of the "gremlin-fest" they're in the midst of. But for most people, that would be the kind of thing you'd share *after the fact*, after you've gained perspective and wisdom. You want to make sure that your audience retains their sense of confidence in you!

For example, one person whose list I was on revealed a lot of chaos in her business and personal life—with the intention of being transparent. I admit, I read everything she wrote. It was kind of like watching a train wreck in slow motion. But what I was reading made me very clear that I would never buy anything from her, nor would I even want to collaborate with her as a joint-venture partner. So keep the transparency balanced. Don't lie or anything. But be conscious about the best times to reveal things. Your readers want to be able to trust you.

Whatever you do share with your audience, make sure it's real. People can detect fake authenticity a mile away. Have you ever seen an email come into your inbox with the subject line, "I'm feeling really vulnerable." Blech! Remember what I said about *showing*, not *telling*? If you're truly sharing something vulnerable, that will come in the telling of it. It's *you* that your audience wants to get to know. So let it be the real you.

If you feel uncomfortable sharing personal stories with your audience, start with baby steps and see how it goes. Stretch a little and gauge the reaction. I'm a very private person, and I avoided sharing anything personal for a long time. I spent two months traveling across Europe with my son in 2007, and I didn't even mention it to my audience. When I lived in Italy for six months, I felt the same pull to just keep it to myself. But I made myself write about the experience, and I discovered how much it meant to my readers. And I had to admit, it was really fun!

It helps to write like you're writing to a friend. Hopefully, after all the work you did to identify your audience—and identify *with* them—you already feel friendly toward them. Be natural, conversational. Make humorous asides, if that's what you do when you're hanging out and having a drink with friends.

When you get personal with your audience, you'll experience a deeper relationship with them—and greater success in your business. Together, your expertise and *you* shine possibility onto your audience. You're their lighthouse. And you know what? When storms hit your business—whether in the form of a pandemic or something else—your audience will return the favor and be *your* lighthouse. Read on and let's explore that in our final chapter.

ACTION MOMENT

1. List two stories from your life you could share with your audience.
2. How might each of those two stories suggest a metaphor for teaching your audience?

Chapter 12
WHEN YOUR AUDIENCE SAVES YOU

*"The best way to find yourself is to
lose yourself in the service of others."*
—MAHATMA GANDHI

SMALL STORMS are always just on the horizon for small business owners, occasionally coming to shore. A web designer goes AWOL, and you can't access your website. Your website or Facebook account gets hacked. A supplier or service provider goes out of business. You make a big mistake on your sales page. These things happen.

You're a business owner, so you roll with the punches, learning and growing from your experiences and your mistakes. When you have a strong, value-providing relationship with your online audience, they roll right along with you. They giggle when your "Oops!" email lands in their inbox, knowing that mistakes happen and you're still trustworthy. They'll even alert you if something is off, like if they start seeing odd messages coming out of your Instagram account.

Now take a bird's-eye view of yourself and your business, and see how that well-nurtured online audience saves you from the confines of an office. It saves you from having to work for awful bosses. It saves you from limits on your income-earning potential. It saves you from being a best-kept secret. It saves you from the sadness of never discovering your voice and your purpose.

You give them value and care in your ways; they reciprocate by buying from you and caring in their ways. It's a mutually caring relationship.

But what about when an unexpected tsunami hits? A tsunami like serious illness.

A Cancer Journey

When Natalie Tollenaere was diagnosed with breast cancer, she had to stop working with her audience—expats transitioning into and out of Africa—to go through the treatment.

> *"The highlight of those very difficult months is that I didn't lose contact with my community. (It even grew bigger!) It made me feel so good. Even ill, I could still keep in touch. I could still be an inspiration and be useful to people who read me! What a great feeling when you feel so down."*

Natalie's experience demonstrates not only the value of having a relationship with her audience, but also of having her audience-building set up and able to operate despite her absence.

Birth After Burnout

I told you the story of my sabbatical year and how my audience made it possible for me to travel for three-quarters of the year. That year, my audience saved my sanity! But what I didn't tell you is what happened *after* that sabbatical year.

I thought that after a year off, and most of it traveling, I'd be raring to get back to work. But when January 2017 rolled around, I *still* wasn't ready to get back to full-heartedly running my business. I couldn't explain why—I just couldn't. I didn't want to travel; I just wanted to be still and pet cats and walk dogs at my local humane society.

My "tsunami" wasn't dramatic. From the outside, it looked like paralysis, but I felt fully at choice. I knew something was going to change; I just didn't know what—or when. So I waited and was quiet. I had faith that whatever "it" was would reveal itself, and I would *know* when it did. I continued to communicate with my list; I offered a few free trainings. My motto was "simple."

And then "it" happened, and I knew it the moment it did. First some background. A few years earlier, I had added some travel-related offers to my product portfolio since I had discovered how much my audience loves to travel. One was a group coaching program to help people develop their online business so that they could travel with it. The other was a program that took people through all the practicalities of how to actually run their business from another country. Between the two of them, however, none of my students or clients ever actually took their business on the road. It was disappointing, and I didn't know how to plug that gap.

Fast forward back to the "it" moment. I was on the phone lamenting this fact to my friend Pam Ivey. She told me about a travel experience she'd had with a group of much-younger entrepreneurs. The company she went with organized groups of business owners to spend a month at a time in cool international destinations. The group lived in apartments close together and got their work done at a local co-working space. And then they had fun exploring the destination.

Pam said, "We need something like this for people our age." (That being 40-plus, wink, wink.)

And that was the eureka moment I'd been waiting for! This is it, I thought. *This* is the missing link, the thing to plug the gap I'd observed. The travel-lovers in my audience didn't want to travel alone, didn't want to try running their business abroad…alone. They wanted to be around other business owners who valued travel as much as they did. They didn't want to go for an extended period with a group of mostly 20-somethings.

Thus was born Adventurous Life International. That conversation was in November 2017. We launched the business in January 2018. All of a sudden, my mojo was back. And my audience loved the concept, with more than three-quarters of our first-year participants coming from my list.

So my audience saved me in two ways. First, they made a second, quieter sabbatical year possible. I used simple emails to my list to sell past programs and the passive-revenue products I had in place. Nothing fancy, no launches, no big effort. Just small and simple. I had consciously contracted my business, yet the relationship I'd built up over the years sustained me.

The second way my audience saved me is in how they responded to my new venture! We took groups to Lisbon, Portugal; Rome, Italy; Ubud, Bali; Barcelona, Spain; Prague, Czechia; and Sydney, Australia. When the coronavirus grounded travel, I just intensified my focus on my relationship marketing portfolio and made more money than in the previous year. My online audience saved me when so many businesses were struggling terribly in the pandemic.

Businesses leaned hard into "virtual" because of the pandemic, making heroic shifts to save not only the business but also the jobs of employees and contractors. The audiences they had nurtured online saved them—and even provided springboards for new growth. And though it may sound a bit dramatic to say that an audience "saved" a business or a job or a person, it actually is that consequential. Here are just a few examples.

Pump It Up

Boxfit, a kickboxing-based fitness club in New Delhi, India, began streaming live classes to save their business and the jobs of 20 employees. So did fitness instructors and yoga studios all over the world. Tribe SF, a San Francisco gym, used Instagram and a Facebook group to promote interest and engagement in the group's workouts, and foster a sense of community. Their audiences came along with them, even grew, now that their market could include the world. Their audiences saved them.

No More Bad Zoom

Before the pandemic, Robbie Samuels had spent a decade establishing his credibility as a networking expert for one-day conferences and association events. As the first wave of lockdowns started rippling through in March 2020, events were canceled, postponed, or moved online, and suddenly the world no longer valued the skill set he had so carefully developed.

Jumping into action, Robbie wrote a quick opt-in gift, "9 Ways to Network in a Pandemic" and started a free weekly

"#NoMoreBadZoom Virtual Happy Hour." He used Zoom virtual breakout rooms for the first time on March 20. By May, he was teaching a four-week program to help presenters improve their Zoom game. His original audience came along with him, and, together with his new audience, propelled him to six figures in eight months as a virtual event design consultant and executive Zoom producer. His audience saved him.

Italy à la Virtual

Anne Robichaud grew up in Wisconsin but has lived in Italy for nearly 50 years, farming, raising children, and giving guided tours of hilltop towns in the Umbria region. Pre-pandemic, Anne conducted close to 100 of these in-person tours each year, and she's one of TripAdvisor's highest-ranking favorites. But like my own travel company, the coronavirus gutted Anne's business.

"I knew I was going to have to reinvent myself," she says.

So, beginning in June 2020, Anne started presenting hour-long *virtual* tours, with themes such as, "Living the Many Splendors of Orvieto" and "Assisi's Medieval Street Art: From the Sacred to the Grotesque" and "Italy's Islands of Refuge." Today her bimonthly virtual tours routinely generate audiences of at least 100 and sometimes as many as 150.

I've attended some of Anne's virtual tours, and they are *packed* with historical, cultural, artistic information and images. It takes generally more than 80 hours to create each presentation, something she says she does with "*grande passione!*" Although her virtual tours haven't yet made up fully for her loss of income due to the pandemic, her online audience saved her from having to give up her work of sharing Italy.

Treasure Hunting

Manic Mermaid, an art gallery with a unique gift shop, had to close its storefront due to Covid-19, so it created live Facebook and Instagram shows to allow viewers to shop virtually. It's been a big hit, and the additional income they've brought in helps them support other small businesses by buying more inventory to sell in their shows.

"This success with our Live show has given us a financial breathing room, plus it allows us to continue with our main focus of why we opened the business in the first place—to take care of others," co-owner Janelle Elms said on a Facebook for Business blog post. Their audience saved them, and so many others.

Your Audience

Whatever your business is, whenever it started, whatever stage you are in of audience development—an online audience can help you weather the dangerous storms that may come your way, whether illness, burnout, pandemic, or anything else. Your audience can *save* you.

It's actually a mutually beneficial experience. You, your services, your trainings, your products, all make a difference in the lives of your growing audience. And then your audience makes a difference in yours.

That's real relationship for you....

FREE

ACTION MOMENT

1. Write about a time in your life when you felt constricted, trapped, or barricaded in some way. What strength did you call on to break through?
2. Do you believe that freedom is given to you by others, or made by you? Explain.

CONCLUSION

AT THE BEGINNING OF THIS BOOK, I told of my experience on the flying trapeze platform and how it relates to creating and tending to your online audience—the fear of fully committing, the courage I needed to summon, and, eventually, the leap.

There's a little bit more to the story. As I flew on the trapeze, my hands in a death grip around the bar, I followed the shouted guidance of the instructor to hoist my legs up and swing upside down by my knees.

A trapeze artist jumped off the other side of the rig, coordinating his swing with mine. At his command, I arched backward and outstretched my arms as we sped toward each other. In a split second, I felt his hands on my wrists, squeezed back on his as instructed, and let my legs straighten off the bar.

I had jumped off a platform 35 feet high, swung upside down by my knees, and now I had fully let go in faith that I would be caught. I was. And it was *glorious.* I had conquered my fear, followed instructions, and was feeling unbelievably exhilarated.

You've learned a lot in this book about conquering your fear and letting go in faith. You've gotten instruction on identifying and attracting your perfect audience, using the economy of generosity, and getting your audience to bond with you, buy from you, and stay loyal.

As you prepare to fly in your business, in your audience building, I invite you to commit to developing a substantive, meaningful, personal connection with the people who need what you can give them.

Commit to stepping up for the people just *waiting* for the wisdom, advice, lessons, perspective, strength, and inspiration that *only you* can provide.

Commit to success, to flying toward your dreams.

And then *feel* the exhilarating freedom and adventure that's waiting for you when you build an online following. The freedom to work and create adventures anywhere in the world. The freedom to experience time abundance and financial well-being. The freedom to choose your creative expression—and your adventures—in business and in life.

Feel the freedom. *Live* your adventures.

Whether near or far,
Whether known to me or unknown,
May you be happy.
May you be well.
May you be peaceful.
May you be FREE.

From the Buddhist Metta Prayer (slightly modified).

ADDITIONAL SUPPORT FOR YOU!

REGISTER NOW FOR THE FREE 3-DAY

FREEDOM BUSINESS BOOTCAMP

READ THIS FIRST

To say thank you for reading my book and support your continued learning, I'd love for you to join me at my 3-day "Freedom Business Bootcamp," **April 6–8, 2021**. Get a jump start now to create your freedom business—at no cost whatsoever. It's my gift to you.

→ Go to **www.FreedomBusinessBootcamp.net** to register now.

ACKNOWLEDGMENTS

I DON'T KNOW WHERE I got my entrepreneurial spirit from; no one in my family growing up was a business owner. But I do know where I get my entrepreneurial support from. First, my mother, who has been a big fan since my very first venture in 1993. Thank you, Mom.

I wouldn't be where I am today without three colleagues who have made an indelible mark on my heart and my business. Pam Ivey, who co-founded Adventurous Life with me, is always a pick-me-up with her sunny attitude and youthful spirit. The adventure quotient in my life has doubled since knowing you! Pat Mussieux is an amazing role model and a reliable travel companion who's accompanied me on many adventures. Our morning walks in Buenos Aires still live in my heart. Danny Iny is a friend, mentor, and one of the smartest entrepreneurs I know. Your support and experience—plus the team you've built up at Mirasee—are inspirational.

Thanks also go to Antonio, Mariale, and Carlota, the Avila VA team that jumped into action when I decided to do this book on a very short time frame. Thank you! And to Angela Montano, whose wisdom has supported my path for years, I'm grateful. Thank you also to the team at The Writer's Ally for your flexibility and great work to get this book published.

Finally, to my son. I'm so proud of you, and always have been. Of all the adventures I've had in my life, being your mother has truly been the biggest and best. Watching you grow into the beautiful man and caring partner that you are fills me with joy. Stay free.

BIBLIOGRAPHY

Books

Buckingham, Marcus, and Clifton, Donald O. *Now, Discover Your Strengths*. New York: Gallup, Inc., 2001, 2020

Burg, Bob, and Mann, John David. *The Go-Giver: A Little Story About a Powerful Business Idea*. New York: Portfolio, 2007

Murray, William Hutchison. *The Scottish Himalayan Expedition*. London: J.M.Dent & Sons, 1951

Pressfield, Steven. *The War of Art: Winning the Inner Creative Battle*. New York: Black Irish Entertainment LLC, 2002

Websites

https://blog.google/outreach-initiatives/small-business/celebrate-international-small-business-day/

https://www.socialmediaexaminer.com/clubhouse-app-how-to-get-started/

https://www.viidigital.com/5-real-stories-about-adapting-to-do-business-online/

https://www.affiliatemarketertraining.com/a-few-successful-online-business-stories-to-keep-you-motivated/

https://neilpatel.com/blog/audiences-vs-keywords/

https://dmgonlinemarketing.com/history-of-lead-nurturing/

https://sumo.com/stories/grow-email-list-with-facebook

https://www.campaignmonitor.com/blog/email-marketing/2019/02/how-to-use-instagram-to-grow-your-email-list/

https://www.mailerlite.com/blog/did-you-know-that-you-can-use-instagram-to-grow-your-email-list

https://later.com/blog/newsletter-instagram/

https://upviral.com/instagram-list-building-tips/

https://kajabi.com/blog/6-simple-ways-to-build-your-email-list-on-twitter

https://www.searchenginejournal.com/twitter-lists-create-use/250631/#close

https://meetedgar.com/blog/how-to-use-twitter-to-massively-boost-signups-for-your-email-list/

https://optinmonster.com/9-ways-to-grow-your-email-list-with-social-media/

https://www.allbusiness.com/build-your-mailing-list-with-linkedin-14916-1.html

https://www.linkedin.com/pulse/how-build-targeted-prospecting-list-using-linkedin-sales-kosakowski

https://www.tailwindapp.com/blog/how-to-use-pinterest-to-rapidly-grow-your-email-list

https://jennakutcherblog.com/how-to-use-pinterest-to-grow-your-email-list/

https://bigincomeparadise.com/building-an-email-list-with-pinterest/

https://www.socialmediaexaminer.com/grow-email-list-pinterest/

https://kajabi.com/blog/8-steps-to-building-your-list-through-youtube

https://optinmonster.com/how-to-build-an-email-list-for-your-youtube-channel/

https://xo.agency/how-to-use-youtube-to-build-your-email-list/

https://blog.aweber.com/digital-marketing-2/4-ways-to-grow-your-email-list-with-youtube.htm

https://www.quicksprout.com/how-to-build-an-email-list-on-your-blog/

https://sharethis.com/best-practices/2017/11/3-steps-to-build-and-grow-your-email-list-through-blogging/

https://optinmonster.com/ultimate-guide-to-guest-blogging-strategy/

https://www.lidwellwriting.com/blog/podcast-list-building

http://blog.ironmarkusa.com/social-media-platforms

https://wearesocial.com/digital-2020

https://www.emailisnotdead.com/

https://www.inc.com/benjamin-p-hardy/extreme-generosity-as-your-entrepreneurial-super-power.html

ABOUT THE AUTHOR

LINDA CLAIRE PUIG is a relationship marketing expert helping small business owners develop loyal, engaged subscribers who become clients and customers. Linda has trained thousands of coaches, mental health professionals, consultants, trainers, authors, and experts on building and nurturing their perfect audience. She also provides done-for-you Ready2Go articles to make keep-in-touch content easy and fast.

An award-winning journalist and writer, Linda's articles have appeared in newspapers, magazines, and newsletters throughout the world for nearly 30 years. She is also the author of *The 6-Figure Newsletter*.

Linda credits her own audience with allowing her to travel the globe while running her business. As she shared stories and lessons from the road, her audience revealed that they were also interested in traveling with their business. So, in 2018, Linda co-founded Adventurous Life Int'l to take groups of entrepreneurs 40-plus to destinations around the world to live, work, and travel in community for a month at a time.

Though she grew up in Missouri and Texas, where all of her family still lives, Linda has called California home for more than 20 years. When she's not traveling, she lives in gorgeous Sonoma County. She's the proud mother of Sela Shiloni, a Los Angeles–based photographer, and all manner of dogs catch her eye. Discover more about Linda's Ready2Go products, training programs, and coaching services: 6FigureNewsletters.com.